LIFE 2.0+

UNLOCK YOUR POTENTIAL AND TRANSFORM YOUR LIFE TODAY WITH THE TOP 100 BOOKS.

TUSHAR MEGHANI

Made with ♥ on the Notion Press Platform
www.notionpress.com

Dear Mom and Dad, Uncle and Aunty, and my dear late Nani and Dada,

I cannot express in words how grateful I am to have had your love and support throughout my life. You have always encouraged me to follow my dreams and passions, and this book is a testament to your unwavering belief in me.

Every word written in this book is dedicated to you. You have been my constant source of inspiration and motivation, and I hope this book makes you proud. It is a tribute to the values you have instilled in me and the sacrifices you have made to make me the person I am today.

To my dear friends and all the other people who have supported me in this journey, I want to extend my heartfelt thanks. Your encouragement, feedback, and love have been invaluable, and I could not have done this without you.

This book is more than just a collection of summaries and learnings from the top 100 books in areas of self-help, productivity, philosophy, investing, business, biography, personal finance, and communication. It is a reflection of the values, beliefs, and experiences that have shaped me as an individual.

I hope that this book helps you transform your life in many parameters, just as it has transformed mine. It is my sincere hope that the lessons and insights shared in this book will help you achieve success in all aspects of your life, be it in business, relationships, personal growth, or anything else.

With deepest gratitude and love,

Tushar

Contents

Contents

Contents

Contents

Contents

Contents

Contents

Contents

Contents

Acknowledgements

I am filled with immense gratitude for the unwavering support and tireless efforts of all those who have contributed to the making of this book. Without their help, this project would not have been possible.

My heart overflows with gratitude towards the authors of the top 100 books featured in this collection. Their words have served as a guiding light for me and for countless others on our journeys of self-improvement and personal growth. It is a great honor to be able to bring together the insights and wisdom of such esteemed writers in one place.

I am also grateful for the unwavering love and support of my family and friends. They have been a constant source of encouragement and inspiration throughout this journey, and I could not have done it without them.

Lastly, I want to express my deepest gratitude to my readers. Your interest in this book and commitment to self-improvement and personal growth has been the driving force behind my work. I hope that this book will serve as a valuable resource for you, and that the knowledge and wisdom contained within its pages will help guide you on your own journey.

I have poured my heart and soul into this book, and it is with great pride and emotion that I present it to you. Thank you from the bottom of my heart for being a part of this journey with me.

About Author

Tushar, a motivated and finance-savvy young man from Rajkot, Gujarat, has poured his heart and soul into creating this transformative book. As an undergraduate student with a passion for self-help, productivity, philosophy, investing, business, biography, personal finance, and communication, Tushar has faced his fair share of struggles in acquiring the knowledge needed to succeed in these areas. He realized that many of life's most essential lessons aren't taught in school or college, and that's why he dedicated himself to creating this book.

Through his own experiences and extensive research, Tushar has condensed the key learnings and takeaways from 100 of the best books in each of these areas. He's excited to connect with readers, and help them tap into their true potential and unleash their greatness.

If you're ready to take your life to the next level, this book is for you. It's time to dive in, learn from the expert, and transform your life in ways you never thought possible!

Preface

Welcome to my book, a treasure trove of knowledge and wisdom from the world's most impactful and transformative books. As an avid reader and lifelong learner, I understand the power of books to inspire, educate, and transform lives. It is this understanding that has led me to create this book - a compilation of summaries and key takeaways of the top 100 books in various areas including self-help, productivity, philosophy, investing, business, biography, personal finance, and communication.

In today's fast-paced world, time is a precious commodity, and it is not always possible to read every book that catches our interest. That's why I've taken the time to curate a selection of the most impactful and relevant books in these areas, and distilled their knowledge and wisdom into concise and comprehensive summaries. My goal is to make it easy for readers to gain knowledge and insights from these books without having to spend the time and money to read them all.

I understand that reading can be a valuable and enriching experience, and I hope that my book will inspire and motivate readers to pick up these books and read them in full. But even if that is not possible, my book will give you a good idea of the main ideas and key takeaways of each book, and the learning and insights distilled from the most important points and key takeaways will give you a good sense of what you can gain from reading them.

I have carefully selected these books based on their impact and relevance in today's world, and each summary has been written with the aim of providing a clear and concise understanding of the main ideas and key takeaways from each book. Whether you're a busy professional, a student, or simply someone looking for a way to improve your life, my book is the perfect companion.

I believe that the knowledge and wisdom contained in the pages of these books can be a catalyst for personal and professional growth, and it is with this belief that I have created this book. My goal is to provide a valuable resource for anyone looking to improve their life, and I hope that it will inspire readers to make the most of the knowledge and wisdom contained in these books.

So sit back, relax and dive into the world of books and learning, where the possibilities are endless. I hope you will enjoy my book as much as I enjoyed creating it.

Introduction

Are you ready to transform your life? This book is your ultimate guide to unlocking your potential, achieving your goals, and living your best life. With the summaries and key takeaways of the top 100 books from various fields, including self-help, productivity, philosophy, investing, business, biography, personal finance, and communication, this book is your shortcut to gaining the knowledge and insights that have taken others years to acquire.

Imagine having the wisdom of the world's top thinkers at your fingertips, distilled into bite-sized pieces that you can easily apply to your daily life. This book provides just that – it's like having a personal coach, mentor, and motivator all in one. Whether you're looking to boost your productivity, develop a growth mindset, or improve your financial literacy, this book will provide the tools and knowledge you need to succeed.

By reading this book, you will discover the secrets of successful people, gain a deeper understanding of the world around you, and unlock your own potential. You will learn the most valuable lessons from the most influential books ever written, and you will be empowered to make positive changes in your life.

So why wait? Your journey towards a better life starts here. Let this book be your guide and take the first step towards your transformation.

CHAPTER I

"The Worry Trick: How Your Brain Tricks You Into Expecting he Worst and What You Can Do About It" by David A. Carbonell.

"The Worry Trick" helps readers understand and manage their problems. Clinical psychologist and anxiety disorder expert David A. Carbonell wrote the book. He founded anxietycoach.com and wrote several books on anxiety.

The book's concept is that concern is a brain illusion that doesn't reflect reality. According to the author, fears are imagined ideas and images, not predictions. He believes the brain's tendency to focus on negative thoughts might cause anxiety and worry.

CBT, acceptance-based therapies, and mindfulness meditation are used to manage stress and anxiety in the book. It also offers games and worksheets to help readers identify and overcome their concerns and tips for adopting a more positive outlook.

The book is meant to help persons with worry and worries as well as those who want to understand and control it. The book is meant to supplement professional treatment for anxiety and concern, not replace it.

The book's takeaways and life lessons are :

• Learn to distinguish between healthy and unhealthy worrying, concern, and anxiety. Learn to identify normal from excessive concern.

• Challenge and change your thinking about your fears to break the cognitive and behavioural patterns that cause your anxiety.

• Find the "safe space" in your mind where you may put your anxieties when they arise and return to them at a more focused and productive time.

• Use mindfulness and other relaxation techniques to reduce the physical and mental impacts of worry.

• Problem-solving and decision-making skills will help you eliminate anxiety.

• Learn how to track and set realistic goals for concern management.

• Learn about self-compassion and how to be kind to yourself while controlling your worry.

CHAPTER II

"Quiet: The Power of Introverts in a World That Can't Stop Talking" by Susan Cain.

"Quiet: The Power of Introverts in a World That Can't Stop Talking" by Susan Cain was published in 2012. This book discusses introversion, extroversion, and how society treats introverts. The author argues that introverts, who are characterised as shy and quiet, have unique skills and benefits that are often overlooked in a culture that values extroversion and friendliness.

The book begins with Carl Jung, the pioneer in the discipline, who coined the words introversion and extroversion in the early 20th century. The author then discusses how introverts are treated in the business, school, and social life.

The book's main message is that introverts are misunderstood and undervalued in an extroverted culture. The author believes introverts should be encouraged to use their unique qualities, such as in-depth and critical thinking, to realise their full potential.

The book also discusses how technology and the internet have made it easier for introverts to interact with others and converse. The author also advises introverts on how to succeed in a world created for extroverts.

In the concluding chapter, the author advises readers to accept themselves and be proud of their introversion. The author believes introverts have a lot to offer and that society should recognise and honour them. This book calls for an inclusive society where introverts and extroverts can prosper.

"Quiet: The Power of Introverts in a World That Can't Stop Talking" examines introversion and extroversion and how society rewards and treats introverts. The main takeaway from this is that introverts have their own strengths and should be encouraged to use them in a culture that values extroversion.

The book's takeaways and life lessons are :

• Recognize that introversion is not a weakness.
• Introverts should be valued for their talents. They can think profoundly and independently, like isolation and silence, and build genuine connections.
• Create an introvert-friendly environment by offering quiet spaces, reducing distractions, and allowing time for reflection.
• Respect introverts' need for quiet and isolation, give them time to think and talk, and let them work independently.
• Recognize the importance of moderation, the value of both extroverted and introverted types, and the truth that a healthy, productive society needs both.
• Recognize that quiet time alone can boost creativity, concentration, and well-being.
• Recognize and value introverts' strengths.

CHAPTER III

"Big Magic: Creative Living Beyond Fear" by Elizabeth Gilbert

Elizabeth Gilbert wrote "Big Magic: Creative Living Beyond Fear," a 2015 self-help book. This book is for creative people who struggle with anxiety, self-doubt, and insecurity. The author discusses how to overcome these barriers and unleash one's creative potential based on her personal writing experiences. The author uses her writing experience.

Six chapters cover different creative expression topics in the book. Gilbert introduces "vast magic" in her first chapter. She calls "big magic" the inexplicable and unpredictable force that drives creativity. She believes everyone can access this magic, but anxiety and self-doubt may make it difficult.

Gilbert discusses creativity, inspiration, perseverance, and fear in the following chapters. She encourages readers to harness their natural curiosity and be open to new ideas. She also emphasises risk-taking and accepting defeat.

The author describes her struggles and how she overcame them. She also suggests making time for creativity, surrounding oneself with supportive people, and being open to inspiration. Gilbert underlines throughout the book that creative pursuits should be used for self-expression, not fame or fortune.

This book teaches that everyone can be creative. Gilbert claims that everyone can access it. She encourages others to overcome self-doubt and embrace their creative potential

by living boldly and authentically.
"Big Magic: Creative Living Beyond Fear" offers suggestions on how to unleash one's creative potential and overcome fear, self-doubt, and uncertainty. The author urges readers to be curious, take risks, and see their creativity as self-expression. Creativity is innate and available to everyone.

The book's takeaways and life lessons are:

- Understand the difference between introversion and shyness and that introversion is a natural personality trait, not a weakness.
- Introverts can think deeply and independently, prefer solitude and silence, and make meaningful connections.
- Create an introvert-friendly environment by offering quiet spaces, reducing distractions, and allowing time for reflection.
- Respect introverts' need for quiet and isolation, give them time to think and talk, and let them work independently.
- Recognize the importance of moderation, the value of both extroverted and introverted types, and the truth that a healthy, productive society needs both.
- Recognize that quiet time alone can boost creativity, concentration, and well-being.
- Recognize and value introverts' strengths.

CHAPTER IV

“The Things You Can See Only When You Slow Down: How to be Calm and Mindful in a Fast-Paced World” by Haemin Sunim

"The Things You Can See Only When You Slow Down: How to be Calm and Mindful in a Fast-Paced World" is Haemin Sunim’s 2017 self-help book. This mindfulness and meditation guide helps readers find inner peace in a fast-paced world. As a Zen Buddhist monk and teacher, the author shares his tips for cultivating mindfulness and compassion. The author shares his personal insights.

This book covers mindfulness and meditation in four parts. This chapter introduces mindfulness and how it can help readers become more aware of their thoughts, feelings, and surroundings. He also provides practical advice on how to meditate, practise breathing exercises, and keep a diary.

In the second section, the author discusses modern compassion and empathy. He believes compassion reduces stress and anxiety and is essential to happiness and well-being. He suggests kindness, forgiveness, and gratitude to increase compassion.

The book’s third chapter emphasises self-care and self-compassion. To maintain a healthy balance between work, rest, and play, the author recommends self-compassion and self-care. He also advises on healthy ways to handle stress and negative emotions.

The book concludes with advice on maintaining mindfulness and compassion in turbulent times. The

author advises readers to be flexible and accept change as a part of life. He also advises on finding life's meaning.
"The Things You Can See Only When You Slow Down" is a mindfulness and meditation handbook that helps readers find peace and happiness in a fast-paced world. This Book teaches mindfulness and meditation. As a Zen Buddhist monk and teacher, the author shares his tips for cultivating mindfulness and compassion. The author provides his personal insights. The most significant lessons are practical tips on how to incorporate mindfulness, compassion, self-care, self-compassion, and flexibility into daily life, how to balance work, rest, and play, and how to find purpose and meaning in life.

The book's takeaways and life lessons are:

• Practice meditation, yoga, journaling, and walking to increase awareness.

• Slow your thoughts, focus on your breath, and notice your thoughts and feelings without judgement.

Learn to let go of past regrets and future anxieties and live in the present.

•Kindness and compassion build empathy, self-compassion, and understanding.

•Mindfulness and introspection help one find inner peace.

•Mindfulness can help you manage stress, anger, and worry.

• Use mindfulness to appreciate the beauty and richness of everyday life and find joy in the seemingly unimportant.

• Practice mindfulness in relationships and cultivate compassion, empathy, and understanding.

CHAPTER V

"The Power of Habit: Why We Do What We Do in Life and Business" by Charles Duhigg

Charles Duhigg's 2012 book "The Power of Habit: Why We Do What We Do in Life and Business" is non-fiction. This book explores the science of habit formation and how it can be applied to personal and professional life. The author uses research and real-life examples to demonstrate how habits are formed, adjusted, and affect our behaviour and decision-making.

The book has three main sections. The author begins by explaining the science and neurobiology of habit formation. He believes that habits are established patterns executed automatically in response to specific cues and that habit formation is an iterative process involving success and failure. The basal ganglia, which helps form habits, is also covered.

In the second half of this article, the author investigates how habits affect personal and professional behaviour and decision-making. He uses real-life examples to show how routines can improve productivity, stress, and addiction. He emphasises self-control and willpower in forming new habits and breaking old ones.

The article concludes with concrete advice for changing routines. He suggests identifying the cues and rewards that produce habits and replacing them with a new behaviour that provides the same benefits. He also advises on self-control, willpower, and habit-change environments.

and supporting others.
This book teaches readers how to increase self-love and optimism to live a successful and fulfilling life. The author shares his personal experiences and practical advice on how to overcome negative ideas and feelings, build self-worth, and focus on the present. The most important thing one can learn from reading this book is that self-love is the foundation of a successful and fulfilling life, and that by developing self-love and optimism, one may build a firm sense of self-worth and live a full life.

The book's takeaways and life lessons are:

- Accept yourself and let go of self-criticism.
- Learn to love and care for yourself as you would a friend. Self-gifting is the finest.
- Learn to set limits and communicate your requirements.
- Always be aware of and take responsibility for your ideas and feelings.
- Learn how to be grateful for what you have.
- Set goals and strive towards them.
- Learn how to create a positive, supportive environment and surround yourself with positive, motivating individuals.
- Use positive affirmations and visualisation to construct your ideal life.

CHAPTER VII

“The Subtle Art of Not Giving a F*ck: A Counterintuitive Approach to Living a Good Life” by Mark Manson.

2016 self-help book "The Subtle Art of Not Giving a F*ck: A Counterintuitive Approach to Living a Good Life" by Mark Manson. 2016 was Manson’s book year. The book recommends focusing on what matters and letting go of the rest, a counterintuitive approach to living well. The author argue that our society’s focus on positivity and happiness is misplaced and that we need a more practical and pragmatic approach to life.

In the book’s first few chapters, the author argues that our society’s overemphasis on positivity and happiness leads to feelings of inadequacy and failure. He advises readers to ignore the unimportant and focus on the important.

The author provides actionable advice on how to handle negative emotions, overcome limiting beliefs, and organise and prioritise goals. He also advises readers to embrace uncertainty and failure as part of life and use them to grow.

The book’s final chapters discuss the importance of finding purpose and taking responsibility for one’s actions. He emphasises living authentically and not caring what others think.

The book’s most important lesson is to focus on practicality and realism rather than positivity and happiness, which can lead to feelings of inadequacy and failure. The author advises readers to focus on what matters, including accepting failure and uncertainty as natural parts of life, taking responsibility for one's actions and choices, and finding purpose and meaning in life.

This book encourages readers to prioritise what matters and let go of the rest. The book proposes this paradoxical way to live well. The author believes that positivism and happiness are misplaced and that a more practical and pragmatic approach to life is needed. The most important thing to take away from this is that a more realistic and pragmatic approach to life is needed and that a good life can be led by letting go of things that don't matter, focusing on things that do, welcoming failure and uncertainty, accepting responsibility for one's actions and decisions, and cultivating a sense of purpose and meaning.

The book's takeaways and life lessons are:

- Be more selective about where you spend your time and energy and focus on what matters to you.
- Identify and rank your most critical values and goals to guide your time and resource allocation.
- Accept that life is difficult and uncertain, and work on overcoming hardship and growing from your experiences.
- Stop trying to be perfect and start being honest with yourself and others.
- Give up the impulse to control everything and work on being more accepting of yourself and others.
- Try new perspectives, laugh, and don't take life too seriously.
- Focus on the journey, not the end, and take pride in your job.
- Instead of avoiding or stifling negative feelings and experiences, learn to use them to grow.

CHAPTER VIII

"Ikigai: The Japanese Secret to a Long and Happy Life" by Hector Garcia and Francesc Miralles.

Hector Garcia and Francesc Miralles wrote "Ikigai: The Japanese Secret to a Long and Happy Life" in 2017. The authors interviewed people of Okinawa, a Japanese island known for its high life expectancy and low lifestyle-related disease rates, to study ikigai and its relevance to modern life.

This book covers ikigai in several chapters. Ikigai is introduced and contrasted with Western notions of happiness and purpose. They then discuss ikigai's four main components: what you're good at, what the world needs, what you're enthusiastic about, and what you can get compensated for.

The writers provide practical advice on identifying and incorporating ikigai into daily life. They also emphasise the importance of good physical and mental health, strong social connections, and a feeling of community for a successful and happy existence.

This book's most significant lesson is that ikigai, or purpose, is needed for a long and happy life. The writers explain how to find and use ikigai.

The book emphasises that ikigai is about finding a balance between doing what one loves, what one is skilled at, what the world needs, and what one can get paid for.

This book features Okinawans, recognised for their longevity and low rate of lifestyle-related disorders, as examples and insights from people who have successfully used ikigai. The authors also examine ikigai's cultural and historical significance in Japan.

The authors highlight the importance of physical and mental health, social interactions, and community, as well as how to find and use one's ikigai. Ikigai, a sense of purpose and meaning in life, is necessary for a long and happy life.

The book's takeaways and life lessons are:

• Discover how ikigai may give your life purpose, meaning, and fulfilment.

• Examine your hobbies, abilities, values, and world's needs to find your ikigai.

• Learn how to incorporate ikigai into your daily life by trying new things, volunteering, or changing careers.

• Learn how to build community, belonging, and connection, which are essential to a fulfilling existence.

• Learn how to eat well, exercise regularly, and manage stress.

• Practicing gratitude, mindfulness, and positive thinking can help you maintain a positive view.

• Let go of future worries and past regrets to live in the present.

• Appreciate the simple things in life and the natural and man-made wonders around you.

CHAPTER IX

“Deep Work: Rules for Focused Success in a Distracted World” by Cal Newport.

"Deep Work: Rules for Focused Success in a Distracted World" is a nonfiction book about how "deep work" might help you succeed in today’s fast-paced, digital world. The author believes that the ability to concentrate and participate in "deep work," which requires intense focus and concentration, is becoming increasingly rare and desirable in today’s culture and can lead to greater success and productivity.

The book’s opening chapter defines "deep work" and analyses its importance in today’s economy and society. In today’s knowledge economy, deep work allows people to create useful work others can’t. One reason the knowledge economy is growing is this. He also notes that "deep work" is becoming obsolete due to the internet and other modern technologies that make it easier to multitask.

The author then provides practical advice on deep work development. He advises eliminating distractions, setting goals for "deep work," and scheduling regular sessions. He also recommends using the Pomodoro Technique, which needs 25-minute focused intervals, to enhance productivity and focus during deep work.

The author also emphasises the importance of work-life balance and the negative effects of frequent diversions and multitasking on productivity and well-being. He stresses that taking time off from work and doing fun things is

essential to mental and physical wellbeing.
The author provides advises on how to include intense work into one's everyday routine and use technology to boost productivity. He advises against using phones or laptops for amusement or distraction when working hard. Instead, use technology purposefully.
The most important thing to take away from this book is that the ability to concentrate and participate in "deep work" is becoming increasingly rare and precious in today's culture and that developing and perfecting this talent can lead to greater success and productivity. The author suggests setting goals, creating a timetable, eliminating distractions, and maintaining a good work-life balance to develop deep work skills. The book also emphasises using technology to support "deep work" rather than detract from it.

The book's takeaways and life lessons are:

- Learn what "deep work" is and how it can help you succeed in our fast-paced, distracted environment.
- Focus on one activity at a time, set aside time each day for deep work, and remove distractions to increase your deep work capacity.
- Use deep work to succeed in business, academics, and art.
- Set goals, set deadlines, and track your progress to improve self-discipline and focus.
- Practice "deep work" by scheduling time for focused work and prioritising chores.
- Use technology to concentrate and reduce distractions.
- Motivate and focus to overcome procrastination and deep work reluctance. Learn to overcome severe work aversion.
- Work hard yet make time for leisure and fun.

CHAPTER X

“The Power of Now” by Eckhart Tolle.

Eckhart Tolle wrote "The Power of Now: A Guide to Spiritual Enlightenment" in 1997. This book guides readers to spiritual enlightenment and inner serenity by focusing on the present. The author believes that obsessing over the past and future is the main cause of our suffering, and that by focusing on the present, we can overcome our negative thoughts and feelings and find true inner peace.

Each chapter of this book explores a different aspect of living in the present. The author begins by discussing how the mind tends to dwell on the past and future, which can cause discontent in the present. The author provides concrete steps to cultivate mindfulness, awareness, and present-moment presence. He also emphasises the importance of releasing negative thoughts and feelings and the role spiritual practises like meditation and mindfulness play in creating inner peace.

The author also discusses "enlightenment" and how being fully present in one’s life can increase awareness of one’s place in the world. If we focus on the present, we can lose our egos and feel one with the universe, he says.

The book’s most important lesson is that our constant focus on the past and future causes our pain and suffering, and that by focusing on the present, we can overcome our negative thoughts and feelings and find true inner peace. The author provides practical advice on how to practise mindfulness, presence, and letting go of negative thoughts and feelings. The book also explores "enlightenment" and how being fully present in the here and now can lead to a greater awareness of one's place in the world, the ability to overcome ego, and a sense of oneness with everything else. The author believes that obsessing on the past and future is the main cause of our suffering, and that by focusing on the now, we can transcend our negative thoughts and feelings and find true inner peace. The book offers practical advice on how to practise mindfulness and awareness, be present in the moment, let go of negative ideas and emotions, and explore "enlightenment" and how it might help one understand themselves and the world.

The book's takeaways and life lessons are:

• Understand to living in the present may bring calm and joy.
• Meditation and other mindful practises can help you be more present in the moment.
• Recognize and then overcome negative thoughts and feelings.
• Let go of the past and future to focus on the present.
• Learn to silence your mind to find inner peace.
• Learn to appreciate the present and apply it.
• Develop innate wisdom by cultivating inner calm and presence.
• Use this moment to connect with your spirituality.

CHAPTER XI

"Mindset: The New Psychology of Success" by Carol S. Dweck.

"Mindset: The New Psychology of Success" by Carol S. Dweck was published in 2006. This book examines "mindset" and how it affects success and goals. The author claims that our thinking, particularly our growth or fixed mindset, determines our success in life.

This book covers mental attitude in chapters. The author initially discusses "fixed mindset" and "growth mindset" and how they affect success. She argues that those with a fixed mindset think their abilities and intelligence are fixed and can't change, whereas people with a growth mindset think they can improve and grow through hard effort and knowledge.

The author provides specific advice on how to develop a growth mindset and a positive outlook on learning and failure in pursuit of excellence. This book also emphasises perseverance and effort. She uses real-world examples and research to demonstrate how crucial mentality is in school, sports, and business.

The book's most essential lesson is that our mindset determines our achievement in life and that persons with a development mindset are more likely to succeed than those with a fixed perspective. The author offers advice on developing a "development mentality" and an optimistic outlook.

The book emphasises the necessity of creating a growth mindset in children and students and the responsibility of parents, educators, and coaches in helping them develop a positive attitude towards learning and failure. The author uses anecdotes and research to show how mentality affects success in education, sports, and business.

The author also believes that persons with a fixed mindset avoid challenges, give up quickly, consider their efforts worthless, ignore helpful feedback, and feel terrified by others' achievement. However, those with a growth mindset are more likely to seek out challenging jobs, keep trying even when they fail, see effort as a method to improve, learn from criticism, and be motivated by others.

The author believes that our mindset—fixed or growth—determines our success in life and provides practical suggestions on how to build a growth mindset, create a positive attitude towards learning and failure, endure in the face of adversity, and nurture a growth mindset in children and students.

The book's takeaways and life lessons are:

- With an open mind, learn about fixed and evolving mindsets and how they affect our ability to succeed.
- Learn how to develop a growth mindset by accepting new challenges, learning from past mistakes, and persevering through hardship.
- Change your limiting self-talk and beliefs.
- Encourage your curiosity and passion for learning.
- Use feedback to grow and implement what you've learnt.
- Growth mindsets can boost resilience and emotional intelligence.
- Learn how to give importance to your life .
- Praise and affirmation can boost self-esteem and motivation.

CHAPTER XII

“Atomic Habits: An Easy & Proven Way to Build Good Habits & Break Bad Ones” by James Clear.

"An Easy and Proven Way to Build Good Habits and Break Bad Ones" is James Clear’s 2018 self-help book. The book focuses on habit development and how small changes to our routines can improve our quality of life. Scientific data and real-world experiences are used to provide meaningful recommendations on how to form good habits and break negative ones.

Chapters cover several aspects of habit building. The author begins by discussing how routines affect human behaviour. He then explains how habits form, including the four rules of behaviour modification (cue, craving, response, and reward).

The author then offers advice on how to develop good habits and break bad ones. This advice suggests making small, progressive changes to our habits, creating an environment that encourages goal-setting, and staying motivated with rewards and personal accountability. He also advises on how to overcome obstacles to habit change, such as procrastination and apathy.

Atomic Habits, a self-help book, discusses habit creation and how small changes can improve our lives. The book’s title refers to the theory that "atoms" form habits. The author provides practical advice on how to develop good habits and break bad ones, based on scientific study and personal experience. He also emphasises the importance of knowing our identities and how they affect our routines. He suggests that focusing on who we want to be can help us form habits that mirror that identity.

The book's takeaways and life lessons are:

• Slowly changing one's behaviour over time is better than trying to alter everything at once.
• The "four laws of behaviour change"—cue, craving, response, and reward—help form new habits and destroy old ones.
•Procrastination and a lack of motivation can be solved by building an environment that supports your goals, employing rewards and accountability to stay motivated, and setting up a supportive environment.
• Focus on building good habits and eliminating bad ones to start a self-improvement feedback loop.
• Accept setbacks and mistakes as part of progress.
• Recognize the relationship between your routines and who you are, and focus on the kind of person you want to be to build routines that match that identity.
• Practice mindfulness and self-reflection to understand what drives your habits.
• Reward yourself for growth and consistency, no matter how gradual or small.
• Ask friends, family, or professionals for help if you can't change your habits.

CHAPTER XIII

Make Your Bed: Little Things That Can Change Your Life...And Maybe the World" by Admiral William H. McRaven.

Former Navy SEAL Admiral William H. McRaven wrote "Make Your Bed: Small Things That Can Transform Your Life...And Maybe the Planet". He applies his military life lessons in this book.

Make your bed first thing. Early morning accomplishments set the tone for the day. He says a schedule organises your life.

Second, find a mentor. The author stresses the significance of friends, family, and mentors to help each other through life's obstacles. He emphasises community service and role modelling.

Thirdly, judge a person's heart, not their flippers. The author recommends readers to choose honesty and sincerity over attractiveness. He emphasises respect and kindness.

Fourth, realise that life is unfair and that you will frequently experience severe setbacks. The author advises readers to view failure as a learning experience. Despite setbacks, he emphasises tenacity and resilience.

Fifthly, learn from others' mistakes. The author advises readers to learn from others and avoid their mistakes. He also stresses humility and learning from others.

The sixth piece of advice is to forgive wrongdoers but remember their life lessons. The author advises readers to forgive others for their mistakes and use their lessons to improve themselves.

The book's takeaways and life lessons are:

• The author suggests starting the day with a small accomplishment, such as making your bed, to motivate you for bigger tasks. Cleaning the kitchen is one.
• The author emphasises working together and having a strong support system, so find someone to help you paddle. He advises readers to surround themselves with people who will support them and celebrate their successes.
• Instead of dwelling on past mistakes, the author advises readers to get over being a sugar cookie and move forward.
• By telling readers to "don't back down from the sharks," the author encourages them to stand up for themselves.
• Sometimes you must plunge headfirst into an obstacle: The author suggests that sometimes the best way to overcome an obstacle is to face it head-on and with determination. Sometimes the best way to overcome an obstacle is to face it head-on.
• The author emphasises the importance of taking risks and not being afraid to fail by saying "don't be afraid to fail." He advises readers to use their mistakes to grow.
• "Stand up to the bullies" is the author's advice to readers.
• Accept new challenges: The author advises readers to accept new challenges.
• Never, ever quit: The author stresses the importance of perseverance and never giving up.

CHAPTER XIV

“Win Your Inner Battle : Defeat the Enemy within and Live Wtih Purpose” by Darius Foroux.

"Win Your Inner Battle" is a self-help book that helps readers overcome internal obstacles and live a meaningful life. "Understanding the enemy within," "Taking action," and "Living with Purpose" are the book’s three main sections.

Darius Foroux defines the "inner adversary" as negative ideas, worries, and uncertainties that prevent us from attaining our goals in the first chapter. He says this inner opponent may be tamed and vanquished with adequate concentration. He emphasises that the inner enemy is within us and that we give it power. He explains how procrastination, self-doubt, perfectionism, and many other behaviours can be the inner adversary.

Foroux provides actionable solutions for overcoming one’s inner enemy and moving forward in the second segment. He emphasises setting clear, quantifiable goals, creating a plan to achieve them, and working consistently towards them. He also emphasises self-discipline, defined as the ability to fulfil duties regardless of emotion. He suggests a morning routine, avoiding distractions, and other ways to develop self-discipline. He also advises readers to have a "growth mentality" and be open to learning, change, and failure.

Foroux emphasises living a meaningful life at the conclusion. He says having a purpose is vital for long-term

training. He provides first-person accounts and thorough case studies of people who used their subconscious thoughts to improve their lives.

Understanding and training the subconscious mind can bring success, prosperity, and happiness, according to the author. The book urges readers to let go of the past and embrace good thoughts and beliefs for a better future through practical exercises and techniques for programming the subconscious mind.

The book's takeaways and life lessons are:

- Properly using the subconscious mind can help us attain our goals and improve our lives.
- The subconscious mind can manifest positive thoughts and beliefs.
- Visualization, affirmations, and repetition harness the subconscious mind.
- To succeed, one must trust the subconscious mind.
- To succeed, positive ideas and emotions must replace negative ones, which restrict the subconscious mind.
- The subconscious can overcome anxieties, phobias, and limiting beliefs.
- Programming the subconscious mind improves health, prosperity, and relationships.
- The subconscious mind can help one achieve happiness and fulfilment.
- Meditation, visualisation, and self-reflection help strengthen the subconscious mind.
- One must be constant and persistent to harness the subconscious mind's potential.

CHAPTER XVI

"The Compound Effect : Jumpstart Your Income, Your Life, Your Success" by Darren Hardy.

Former Success Magazine publisher Darren Hardy wrote "The Compound Effect" in 2011. The book's main idea is that small, consistent efforts can lead to big results in personal and professional life. Hardy advises focusing on daily routines and incremental improvements to succeed. Over time, these small changes can change a person's life.

This book has three parts: The Compound Effect, Momentum, and Direction. In the book's first section, Hardy explains the compound effect's science and how it can be applied to health, finances, and relationships. He emphasises persistence and baby steps to achieve big goals. In the following section, Hardy discusses the significance of momentum, which can be defined as the driving force that propels us forward in spite of challenges. He contends that when we are actively engaged in something, we are less likely to give up and more likely to prevail in spite of the challenges we face. He also tells us how to build momentum by taking a series of small steps towards our goals in a planned way.

Hardy emphasises the significance of being able to point one's life in a specific direction throughout the conclusion of the book. He contends that in the absence of a definite path, it is easy to become preoccupied with the immediate matters at hand and to lose track of the long-term objectives we have set for ourselves. In addition to that, he discusses how to plan for and accomplish one's objectives by employing a methodology known as SMARTER, which stands for Specific, Measurable, Attainable, Relevant, and Time-bound.

In summary, the book is titled "The Compound Effect." The book provides a clear and concrete method for accomplishing goals and encourages the reader to focus on daily habits and routines that lead to gradual gains. People who want a step-by-step strategy to success would like this book.

The book's takeaways and life lessons are:

- The "compound effect" suggests that repeating small actions can lead to big results.
- Starting little and staying persistent is better than trying to make big changes overnight.
- The author emphasises setting specific goals, tracking progress, and recognising even little achievements.
- To succeed, one should create positive habits and break negative ones, focus on what one can control and let go of what one cannot, and take responsibility for one's actions and decisions.
- The author also emphasises self-discipline, tenacity, and patience as keys to success.
- The author advises the reader to think about their perfect future and take daily steps towards their goals.
- The author advises readers to accept progress as natural and to use setbacks to improve.
- The author concludes that daily action and improvement are important, even if they are small.

CHAPTER XVII

"Why "A" Students Work For "C" Student : Rich Dad's Guide to Financial Education for Parents" by Robert T. Kiyosaki

Robert T. Kiyosaki's "Why A Students Work for C Students" examines the gap between traditional education and the real world of money and business. This book targets "C" students. Kiyosaki's personal experiences and insights are used in the conversational book. The book targets parents and educators.

The first chapter of this book discusses the traditional educational system and its restrictions on students. Kiyosaki claims that the traditional educational system produces "A" students who excel in school but are unprepared for the real world of money and business. Because the traditional educational system focuses on "A" students, he says. He claims that "A" students are told to work hard, get good grades, and behave well, while "C" students are told to think for themselves, be creative, and take risks.

After that, Kiyosaki discusses the importance of financial education and how most colleges don't teach it. He believes that financial literacy can be taught and practised by anyone who wants to succeed in life. He believes parents should teach their children about saving, spending, and investing from a young age.

This book also discusses self-awareness and knowing one's strengths and weaknesses. Kiyosaki emphasises maximising one's strengths and improving one's weaknesses. He also stresses the importance of building a well-rounded team by surrounding oneself with varied strengths and shortcomings.

It stimulates creative thinking and early money and investment education. It encourages creativity. It also emphasises the importance of self-awareness, including understanding one's strengths and weaknesses, and surrounding oneself with people who have different mixes of these traits.

The book's takeaways and life lessons are:

- The book emphasises that financial education is as important as traditional education and should be taught in schools and homes.
- Assets, like rental properties, make money, while liabilities, like credit card debt, take it away. The author also says assets appreciate over time.
- Self-sufficiency The author emphasises financial independence and not relying on a steady wage or a traditional job path throughout the book.
- This book encourages readers to start businesses and become entrepreneurs to achieve financial freedom.
- Calculated risk-taking The book teaches readers to take calculated chances and not be afraid of failure to succeed financially.
- Encourage kids to start businesses.
- Teach your pupils about assets and obligations.
- Encourage children to take reasonable risks and learn from their errors.
- Teach kids about financial freedom and not relying on a steady paycheck.

CHAPTER XVIII

“Rich Dad Poor Dad” by Robert Kiyosaki.

"Rich Dad, Poor Dad" by Robert Kiyosaki discusses personal finance. Kiyosaki’s "rich dad" was his best friend’s father, and his "poor dad" was himself. The biography recounts Kiyosaki’s financial lessons from his "rich dad" and "poor dad" (his biological father).

This book covers many financial themes, including how vital it is to understand money, how to distinguish assets from liabilities, how valuable it is to gain money without doing anything, and the pitfalls of following traditional financial advice.

One of the most significant concepts this book teaches is the need of knowing money and assets and liabilities. Kiyosaki says assets build wealth, but obligations deplete it. He advises his followers to focus on assets like rental homes or investments that generate passive income immediately.

Developing many financial success paths is another crucial piece of information. In "Rich Dad, Poor Dad," Robert Kiyosaki argues that relying on a single revenue source, such a wage, might place one in a dangerous financial position. He recommends investments and side businesses to help his readers achieve financial freedom.

The book’s takeaways and life lessons are:

- Understand how assets and liabilities produce wealth.
- Learn why financial education and money management

are crucial.

• Think like an entrepreneur and consider non-traditional work possibilities.

• Understand the importance of diversifying your income and investments.

• Take financial risks to succeed.

• Understand the difference between working for and letting money work for you.

• Learn how to invest in businesses and real estate.

• Understand the importance of having a long-term financial strategy and not being affected by market volatility.

CHAPTER XIX

"The Total Money Makeover: A Proven Plan for Financial Fitness" by Dave Ramsey

Dave Ramsey, a financial planner and radio personality, wrote "The Total Money Makeover: A Proven Plan for Financial Fitness." This book teaches step-by-step how to achieve financial freedom and take control of one's finances so one may do what they want with their money.

The book begins with common money blunders including living paycheck to paycheck, carrying credit card debt, and not having a retirement savings plan. Ramsey's six-step plan for financial wellness is presented next:

1. An emergency fund starts with $1,000. The "debt snowball" technique pays off all obligations.
2. A 3-6-month emergency fund is an excellent idea.
3. 15% of income in Roth IRAs and pre-tax retirement plans
4. Investing in the kids' college education, paying off the mortgage early, and being generous with one's wealth
5. Ramsey emphasises budgeting, cutting expenses, and not raising one's level of life to finish these phases. 6. He also emphasises changing one's money mindset and learning to live on less.

The book is mostly on people who followed Ramsey's plan and became financially independent. He also offers motivational tips and exercises.

The book's takeaways and life lessons are:

• Stick to a budget.
• Avoid overspending.
• Eliminate debt quickly.
• Save for emergencies.
• Invest long-term.
• Save instead of borrowing for big purchases.
• Avoid lifestyle inflation.
• Plan to give back and be generous with your wealth, and utilise your money intentionally and productively.

CHAPTER XX

“I Will Teach You to Be Rich” by Ramit Sethi.

Ramit Sethi’s "I Will Teach You to Be Rich" is a personal finance guide that helps readers take charge of their finances and become rich with actionable advice. This book covers budgeting, saving, investing, and several income streams. It also gives readers tasks and examples to apply the topics.

To maximise one’s financial potential, Sethi emphasises automating one’s financial processes and creating simple ways to save and invest money. He also encourages people to set lofty financial goals and act boldly to achieve them. He claims that with a little information and the appropriate mindset, anyone can start building riches. He thinks many people fear they can’t succeed financially because they’re poor.

Sethi explains his life journey, including how he went from a poor college student to a comfortable financial situation, in addition to providing advice. This story shows that anyone can succeed financially if they work hard and make smart decisions.

The book provides a detailed, actionable plan for financial achievement. As such, it is a great resource for anyone interested in financial independence and wealth accumulation.

The book’s takeaways and life lessons are:

- The importance of setting precise financial goals and devising a plan to achieve them
- The power of putting your finances on autopilot by setting up automatic programmes for saving and investing money
- Using tax-favored retirement plans like 401(k)s and IRAs is crucial.
- The importance of investing in assets like stocks and property that have the potential to increase in price, such as those with capital appreciation, the importance of establishing a financial plan and sticking to it, and the benefits of keeping detailed records of one's expenditures.
- The importance of patience, tenacity, and not giving up when things go tough when pursuing financial goals
- The importance of taking charge of one's financial future and actively pursuing it

CHAPTER XXI

“The Psychology of Money : Timeless Lesson on Wealth, Greed And Happiness” by Morgan Hpusel.

"The Psychology of Money" by Morgan Housel examines the complex relationship between financial achievement and subjective well-being. This book’s chapters explore a different aspect of the two parties' relationship.

The book discusses how people have unrealistic ideas about money and what it can do for them. The author says people often think more money will make them happier. The author believes this is not always true.

The book argues that emotions lead people to make poor financial decisions. According to the author, money decisions are frequently based on emotions rather than reasoning.

The book also explores how upbringing and life experiences shape people’s financial views. The author contends that persons who grew up poor may have different views on wealth than those who did not.

The author also examines how aspirations and values affect money attitudes. He believes that people with different goals and values will view money differently.

The book also provides advice on setting financial goals, budgeting, investing, and saving.

"The Psychology of Money" explores the complex relationship between money and happiness in a thought-provoking and intellectual manner. This book shows how to strengthen one’s relationship with money and succeed financially.

The book's takeaways and life lessons are:

• Understanding that our financial life involve feelings, prejudices, and psychology is crucial to financial success.
• acknowledging that our money decisions are often influenced more by our past and society's expectations than by our rationality.
• Understanding that financial success includes awareness of and control over money-related emotions and feelings.
• Financial literacy requires confronting our money beliefs and the societal and cultural narratives that shape them.
• Understanding that financial success is a journey with ups and downs that requires patience, persistence, and a long-term outlook is crucial.
• Happiness is more important than goal-setting.
• Improving financial literacy and decision-making,
• Developing a healthy connection with money and seeing it as a tool to achieve our goals is crucial to financial independence.

CHAPTER XXII

“How to Get Rich” by Felix Dennis.

Felix Dennis’s "How to Get Rich" is a practical guide to financial success. Felix Dennis, the book’s author, became a millionaire through several businesses. He shares his life lessons from business achievement in this book.

This book has three sections: "Getting Rich," "Staying Rich," and "Being Rich." In the first part, Dennis discusses wealth production. He believes that focusing on a goal, taking calculated risks, and overcoming failures are the keys to prosperity. He also emphasises self-discipline and hard work in one’s career.

In the book’s second and final section, "Staying Rich," Dennis discusses prudent wealth management. He emphasises having a solid investing strategy, living within one’s means, and avoiding lifestyle inflation. He advises diversifying income and being open to new opportunities.

"Being Rich," Dennis' third segment, discusses the importance of enjoying one’s money and how it may affect happiness. He believed that true riches were both money and a full life.

"How to Get Rich" is a practical, actionable guide that teaches readers how to get rich and succeed financially. By sharing his journey to becoming a self-made millionaire, the author encourages readers to take control of their finances. He also shares his life lessons.

The book’s takeaways and life lessons are:

- Focusing on a goal is crucial to building wealth.
- Take risks and persevere.
- Avoid lifestyle inflation and spend less than one earns to preserve wealth.
- Income from multiple sources to ensure financial security.
- True prosperity includes financial success and a meaningful life.

CHAPTER XXIII

“The Simple Path to Wealth: Your Road Map to Financial Independence and a Rich, Free Life” by JL Collins

J.L. Collins’s "The Simple Path to Wealth" is a personal finance guide that helps readers achieve financial independence and a rich and rewarding life. Financial blogger JL Collins was a stockbroker. He has written on personal finance for over ten years. He wrote this book about his journey to financial independence from his family.

The book has three main sections. In "The Simple Path," the author describes his personal finance philosophy and the steps needed to achieve financial freedom. The book’s second part, "The Heavy Lifting," details the author’s wealth-building practises. These include saving, investment, and frugality. The third section, "The Freedom Path," discusses how to live a rich and satisfying life after financial independence.

This book emphasises long-term saving and investing. The author advises saving a lot of one’s salary and investing it in a wide portfolio of low-cost index funds to build wealth. The author thinks this generates money best. He also emphasises avoiding lifestyle inflation and living below one’s means to save more.

"F-you money" is another important topic in the book. The author says financial independence means having enough money and assets to leave a job or situation you don’t like. It shows you can make good financial decisions. He also recommends using passive income streams to generate earnings without working. Passive revenue streams demand no work.

The author also advises having a "big why" for financial independence. If you can explain why you want financial freedom, it will be easier to stay motivated and focused.

The book's takeaways and life lessons are:

- Create a budget and follow it.
- Prioritize saving and investing portion of your earnings.
- Cut debt and curb lifestyle inflation.
- Explore ways to make money and learn about money management and the stock market.
- Be patient and long-term when accumulating wealth.
- Balancing enjoying the now with planning for the future

CHAPTER XXIV

"Quit Like a Millionaire: No Gimmicks, Luck, or Trust Fund Required" by Kristy Shen and Bryce Leung

Kristy Shen and Bryce Leung's "Quit Like a Millionaire" teaches financial independence and early retirement. The authors quit their well-known jobs in their 30s to live a life without money, which inspired this book.

The authors start the book by sharing how they became wealthy by living frugally, investing wisely, and focusing on assets that generate income for themselves and their families. They then explained how to become financially independent and retire early.

This book teaches that understanding positive and negative debt is crucial. Mortgages and student loans can be used to finance investments in assets with potential value growth. Credit card and auto loans are used to buy depreciating goods. It can hinder debt repayment and financial independence.

The book also emphasises thriftiness and lifestyle inflation. This suggests that when your income rises, you should resist the urge to spend more and instead invest in assets that generate income.

Investing in low-cost index funds is another important lesson. The authors show that investing in a diversified portfolio of low-cost index funds rather than picking individual stocks or timing the market can yield better returns. A diverse index fund portfolio can achieve this.

This book also discusses the importance of diversifying

income and entrepreneurship in financial independence. The authors explain how multiple income streams can provide a safety net and make financial independence easier.

The writers also cover the significance of establishing a distinct picture in your mind of how you want your life to unfold once you have reached the point where you are financially independent. Among these are the formulation of specific monetary objectives, the formulation of a strategy to realise those objectives, and the monitoring of one's progress towards the goals.

In general, "Quit Like a Millionaire" is a guide that is practical and actionable in nature, and it is geared towards helping readers achieve financial independence and retire at an earlier age. This book is not difficult to read, and it contains a wealth of information and ideas that can be put into practise by anyone who is interested in achieving monetary independence.

The book's takeaways and life lessons are:

- Setting a clear financial goal and making a plan to reach it
- It is very important to understand how time and compound interest affect assets on a basic level.
- keeping an eye on the rising cost of living and striving to cut wasteful expenditures
- Put aside a significant portion of your earnings and put those savings into low-cost index funds.
- Tracking purchases and avoiding debt are crucial.
- Making smart career choices and actively seeking high-paying jobs or starting a business
- Prioritize financial independence and choices that support your long-term goals.

CHAPTER XXV

"The Richest Man in Babylon" by George S. Clason.

The personal finance and wealth-building classic "The Richest Man in Babylon" by George S. Clason. Its wisdom endures. The book uses parables and tales to impart its lessons in ancient Babylon. Arkad, the main character, rises from a poor scribe to Babylon's richest man with the support of his wealthy friends and mentors.

This book shows that saving and investing money is the best method to build wealth. Clason advises living below one's means and saving at least 10% of one's wages to succeed financially. He also stresses the need of investing in revenue-generating assets like real estate or a small business and avoiding income-free investments.

"Pay yourself first" is another key notion in the book. This entails prioritising savings and investment over bills and other expenses. This ensures that you constantly save for your goals instead of living paycheck to paycheck like most individuals.

The novel emphasises education and good advise. Arkad's advisors explain compound interest and warn him about debt. They suggest he study personal finance and investing.

"The Richest Man in Babylon" is a timeless classic that gives practical advice on building wealth and financial independence. The book gives this counsel. By saving and investing, living below their means, prioritising self-payment, and seeking good guidance, anyone may implement their ideas.

The book's takeaways and life lessons are:

• Save and invest at least 10% of your pay for financial success.
• Watch your spending. Live frugally and avoid wasteful expenditures.
•Investing and seeking new opportunities will increase your wealth.
•To prevent theft, watch your possessions.
• Turn your property into a profitable investment: Make money from your home if you own it.
• Guarantee income: Save and invest monthly to secure your retirement.
• Educate yourself and look for ways to earn more.
•Five golden rules: Any guy who gives at least 10% of his wages to build an estate for himself and his family will receive gold in increasing quantities. Gold will willingly labour for a wise owner. Gold will stick to the prudent owner who invests it with advise from wise persons. Gold will slip away from the man who does not save at least 10% of his wages to develop an estate for his family.

CHAPTER XXVI

“The Millionaire Next Door: The Surprising Secrets of America's Wealthy” by Thomas J. Stanley and William D. Danko.

"The Millionaire Next Door: The Surprising Secrets of America’s Wealthy" by Thomas J. Stanley and William D. Danko examines wealthy Americans' habits and personalities. This book surveys and interviews millionaires to understand their money behaviour and opinions. Research underpins the text.

The book’s most essential lesson is that most millionaires don’t show off their wealth. Instead, they are thrifty and value saving and investing over consuming. The authors believe this is one of the key reasons these folks became affluent.

Another important point is that most billionaires are self-made and worked hard to get rich. The authors argue that most billionaires earned their wealth via hard effort. They believe this because most millionaires were not born rich.

The text emphasises the importance of setting a financial goal and creating a plan to achieve it. Having a financial goal, like saving for retirement or paying off debt, is one of the best ways to stay motivated and on track, according to the authors.

The author also emphasises knowing one’s income, expenses, and net worth. This helps people make smart money decisions and track their financial goals, according to the authors.

The book also emphasises the importance of a diverse investment portfolio with stocks, bonds, and property to reduce risk and maximise profits.

"The Millionaire Next Door" provides a glimpse into the lives of wealthy Americans. It emphasises thriftiness, dedication, and hard work in wealth accumulation and offers tips for financial success.

The book's takeaways and life lessons are:

- Live within your means. Affluent people maintain their lifestyles constant by doing this. Living below their means allows them to save and invest more, increasing their lifetime wealth.
- Debt-free: Wealthy people avoid personal debt except when necessary to buy income-generating assets.
- Invest in income-generating assets instead of buying consumer goods or luxury products.
- Wealthy people have long-term financial goals and focus on building wealth over time.
- Save and invest consistently. Successful savers and investors are disciplined and persistent. They know wealth takes time and work.
- Study personal finance and investing. Successful individuals do this, and you should too. They prioritise schooling to enhance their finances and accumulate wealth.

CHAPTER XXVII

“Financial Freedom: A Proven Path to All the Money You Will Ever Need” by Grant Sabatier

Grant Sabatier’s "Financial Independence: A Proven Path to All the Money You Will Ever Need" is a comprehensive guide to financial freedom and wealth. This book is based on the author’s five-year journey from poverty to financial independence. He shares his strategies for financial success, including tips for budgeting, investing, and earning many streams of income.

This book emphasises the necessity to set financial goals and create a plan to achieve them. Sabatier recommends budgeting and tracking spending to recover financial control. He also recommends learning new skills and building a diverse income portfolio to invest in oneself.

The book emphasises compound interest, another key concept. Sabatier shows how early investments can increase exponentially into big fortunes. He also emphasises strategic risk-taking and investing in high-return assets.

The author recommends living below one’s means, negotiating bills and salaries, and automating saves and investing. He also advises readers to build riches slowly rather than quickly.

"Financial Freedom: A Proven Path to All the Money You Will Ever Need" is a practical and exciting guide to financial freedom and wealth. It outlines a strategy, plan, and financial goals. It can help people gain financial management and independence.

The book's takeaways and life lessons are:

•Clear financial goals: Sabatier recommends readers to develop clear, measurable, and achievable financial goals to inspire them.
• Sabatier emphasises diverse revenue streams to reduce risk and maximise earnings. Multiple income streams can achieve this.
• Investing in oneself to boost earnings: Sabatier advises readers to develop their skills, talents, and education to boost their earnings.
• Sabatier emphasises living below one's means to save and invest. Spend less.
• Emergency funds Sabatier advises his readers to set up a six-month emergency fund in case of an emergency.
• Sabatier recommends investing in low-cost index funds to make money over time.
• Measured risks: Sabatier advises readers to take calculated risks to potentially earn more money.
• Fostering support Sabatier stresses the importance of a supporting group of like-minded people who can offer guidance and encouragement throughout the trip.

CHAPTER XXVIII

“The Everything Store: Jeff Bezos and the Age of Amazon” by Brad Stone.

Brad Stone’s book covers Amazon and its founder, Jeff Bezos, in detail. "The Everything Store: Jeff Bezos and the Age of Amazon" was published in 2014. The book chronicles the company’s rise from an online bookstore to one of the world’s most powerful and influential companies.

This book shows how Bezos persistently pursued customer satisfaction from the start. Amazon’s customer-first approach and willingness to experiment and take risks helped it soar to the top of the e-commerce market.

In today’s fast changing technology scene, creativity and flexibility are essential. Amazon’s ability to adapt and develop new products, services, and business models has contributed to its rapid growth and industry leadership.

Jeff Bezos describes his leadership style and Amazon’s unique culture in this book. Innovation, experimentation, and a long-term vision have helped the company recruit and retain top talent.

"The Everything Store" is a must-read for everyone interested in Amazon’s rise and its guiding principles. It provides insight into the strategies and mindset of one of our most successful businesspeople and how they may be applied to any firm or individual’s success.

The book’s takeaways and life lessons are:

The book's takeaways and life lessons are:

• Accept uncertainty and change.
• Promote a risk-taking attitude.
• Look for novel solutions to your problems.
• Promote teamwork and ideas.
• Value creative and technical skills in innovation.
• Monitor emerging industries and technology.
• Keep evolving to stay ahead of the competition.
• Let employees lead innovation in the company.
• Think long-term and stay committed, especially when faced with obstacles.
• Accept that innovation and progress require failure.
• Purpose and values help make decisions.
• Encourage diversity and openness so people can learn from each other.

CHAPTER XXX

Shoe Dog: A Memoir by the Creator of Nike" by Phil Knight.

Shoe Dog is Phil Knight's memoir. The book describes how Knight combined his love of running with his entrepreneurial spirit to create one of the most famous companies in history.

Knight tells how he fell in love with running at the University of Oregon and began experimenting with shoe types. He decided to sell cheap Japanese running shoes in the US.

The book describes the company's early funding challenges, financial losses, and fierce competition from other shoe producers. Knight and his team persevered, innovating and expanding the conceivable. They invented the Swoosh logo, the first "Waffle" sole shoe, and the "Just Do It" slogan, which helped the company rise to fame.

A 1990s workplace scandal and Knight's decision-making and leadership issues arose as the business grew. He never wavered from the business's founding values.

The book offers a fascinating glimpse at business life and one of the most successful companies in history. It's about resilience, tenacity, and how an idea can change history. This book teaches invention, tenacity, goal-setting, and how an idea may change history.

The book's takeaways and life lessons are:

• Persistence: Phil overcame production and budgetary issues in Nike's early years. He recounts his many struggles to make the company profitable.

•Phil Knight gambled to build Nike. Phil took risks by leaving his secure job to start his own company, investing all his money, and borrowing money.

• Phil and his team needed flexibility to stay competitive as the business grew and the industry changed. They tried new business ideas without hesitation.

• Customer focus: Phil emphasises the importance of listening to and understanding customers throughout the book.

• Phil examines how branding and storytelling helped Nike succeed. He worked with his team to create a compelling business brand story and identity.

CHAPTER XXXI

"Leonardo da Vinci" by Walter Isaacson.

Walter Isaacson's Leonardo da Vinci biography covers the Renaissance artist and inventor. The book details Leonardo's life and accomplishments. Isaacson examines Leonardo's science, technology, and art, including the Mona Lisa and The Last Supper. The book details Leonardo's relationships, poverty, and unrecognition.

Isaacson's book examined Leonardo's notebooks and writings, revealing his methods, ideas, and thoughts. The book includes past and present narratives to complete Leonardo's life and contributions.

Leonardo's insatiable thirst for knowledge drives the book. Isaacson discusses how Leonardo's insatiable curiosity led him to study anatomy, botany, and engineering and led to groundbreaking discoveries in each of these fields. The book also examines Leonardo's art and science and how he sought to understand and represent nature in new and innovative ways.

The book also explores Leonardo's impact on modern society. Isaacson claims Leonardo's discoveries and ideas shaped art, science, and technology. They change our perspective. The book shows how Leonardo's work has influenced artists, scientists, and innovators throughout history and continues to inspire people today.

"Leonardo da Vinci" is a fascinating biography of one of history's most important figures. Professionals and laypeople alike will enjoy Isaacson's straightforward writing. The book is fascinating and enlightening about Leonardo's life and work.

The book's takeaways and life lessons are:

• Be curious. Leonardo experimented and observed to satisfy his unquenchable curiosity about the universe.
• Accept failure: Leonardo didn't fear mistakes and utilised them to progress.
• Benefit from hard work. Years of practise and tenacity developed Leonardo's capabilities.
• Recognize the power of creativity: Leonardo was a master, and his works were a mix of talent, experimentation, and imagination.
• Value teamwork: Leonardo collaborated with other artists and scientists, which helped him succeed.
• Accept diversity. Leonardo innovated science and art.
• Accept passion. Leonardo's success was driven by his passion to understand the world.

CHAPTER XXXII

“The Snowball: Warren Buffett and the Business of Life” by Alice Schroeder.

Alice Schroeder’s "The Snowball: Warren Buffett and the Business of Life" is Buffett’s biography. The book explores Buffett’s childhood and how it shaped his investing style. It also examines how he became a top investor.

The book covers Buffett’s early investment interest and upbringing in Omaha, Nebraska. He started investing in stocks at a young age and developed a long-term, value-based strategy. The book also discusses his early economic initiatives, including the 1950s and 1960s collaborations that led to Berkshire Hathaway, his conglomerate.

The book discusses Buffett’s management and leadership styles. It emphasises his lack of direct supervision, his willingness to give his managers authority, and his focus on acquiring and retaining top personnel. His compassion and dedication to society are also mentioned.

In the book, Berkshire Hathaway buys GEICO, Dairy Queen, and Fruit of the Loom. It examines how Buffett found and bought these businesses and made Berkshire Hathaway stockholders so rich.

"The Snowball" covers Warren Buffett’s life and career, providing insight into his investment, management, and leadership styles. Leaders, businesspeople, and investors should read it.

The book’s takeaways and life lessons are:

- Understand compounding's long-term financial benefits.
- Study successful people's habits and strategies.
- Think long-term and value your assets and businesses.
- Learn about the world and its many industries.
- After understanding your financial goals, create a plan.
- Surround yourself with helpful and guiding people.
- Spend and save with patience and self-control.
- Take chances and fair risks.
- Improve and learn from mistakes.

CHAPTER XXXIII

"Einstein: His Life and Universe" by Walter Isaacson.

"Einstein: His Life and Universe" by Walter Isaacson chronicles Albert Einstein's life. The book describes Einstein's academic struggles in Germany and his acceptance to the Swiss Federal Polytechnic in Zurich. It also covers his early scientific work, including special relativity, which revolutionised space and time.

The book covers Einstein's relationships, off-the-shoulder children, and marriages. He also spoke out against Nazism in Europe and immigrated to the US.

The book also discusses Einstein's later scientific achievements, such as his theory of general relativity, which built on special relativity and changed our understanding of gravity. The book discusses his quantum physics and atomic bomb accomplishments.

The book examines Einstein's life and accomplishments as well as his character and personality. It reveals that Einstein was complex and eager to discover the universe's fundamental rules.

Isaacson uses Einstein's contemporaries' insights and personal correspondences to give a unique perspective on the scientist and his work. The book contains some never-before-published photos.

"Einstein: His Life and Universe" is Walter Isaacson's exhaustive, well-researched biography of one of the 20th century's finest minds. It covers Einstein's life, legacy, and personality.

The book's takeaways and life lessons are:

• Be curious like Albert Einstein, who spent his life asking questions and seeking new knowledge.
• Like Albert Einstein, work hard and pursue your goals.
• Like Einstein, challenge your preconceptions and be open to new ideas.
• Be creative and imaginative like Einstein, who visualised and understood complex scientific concepts.
• Like Einstein, blend humility with confidence.
• Laugh and play. Einstein was a witty man who used games and thought experiments to understand complex scientific concepts.
• Problem-solving and creative thinking are crucial, as Einstein was known for his unique approach to issues.
• Like Einstein, persevere through challenges and setbacks.
• Like Einstein, find purpose and meaning in your work.

CHAPTER XXXIV

“Autobiography of a Yogi” by Paramahansa Yogananda.

"Autobiography of a Yogi" was written by Paramahansa Yogananda, a self-realized master and 20th century spiritual luminary. This autobiography covers Yogananda’s childhood in rural India, his search for a teacher, and his travels and teachings in the West. It describes Yogananda’s spiritual awakening, meetings with Indian saints and sages, and self-knowledge.

Chapters cover several periods of Yogananda’s life. The book’s main focus is finding a spiritual guide to self-realization. Yogananda wrote about his gurus and how they helped him grow spiritually. He also recounts his enlightenment and encounters with spiritual leaders.

Meditation and building a strong relationship with God are also taught in the book. Yogananda gives advises on achieving inner peace and overcoming spiritual challenges.

"Autobiography of a Yogi" emphasises the need for a spiritual teacher to help one achieve self-realization. The book emphasises the importance of following the guru’s instructions to grow spiritually. Meditation is recommended for spiritual growth in the book. It emphasises inner joy and tranquilly and how to navigate spiritual challenges.

The book’s takeaways and life lessons are:

• The importance of finding a guru or spiritual guide to help you along the spiritual path • meditation and other spiritual practises to calm the mind and connect with the divine

• The law of karma states that our thoughts and actions affect our present and future feelings.

• The need of giving back and exhibiting compassion as a way to progress spiritually and transcend oneself

• The idea that one can encounter God through any faith and that all religions ultimately point to the same spiritual truths

CHAPTER XXXV

“Steve Jobs” by Walter Isaacson.

Walter Isaacson’s "Steve Jobs" biography covers Apple Inc.’s late co-founder and CEO. The book traces Jobs‘ life from his early years until his 2011 death and gives readers an insight into his innovative and successful business mind. The book covers Jobs’ adoption, childhood in Silicon Valley, and initial experiences with electronics and computers. In college, he met Steve Wozniak, who would later work with him and found Apple.

The book also covers Apple’s history, including the Apple I and II, Macintosh, iPod, iPhone, and iPad. Isaacson extensively covers Jobs’s management style and approaches. He discusses how Jobs valued design and user experience, insisted on secrecy, and inspired and motivated his workers.

Isaacson examines Jobs‘ marriage, children, and pancreatic cancer. He discusses Jobs’ return to Apple after his firing and Apple’s success under his leadership.

The book offers insights into the mindset of a visionary leader and the ideals that Jobs championed and applied at Apple, including design, creativity, a user-centered approach, and his ability to think unconventionally and question the existing quo. As Jobs did throughout his career, it emphasises persistence and the ability to overcome obstacles. It also emphasises the need of a strong team and the ability to lead them towards a goal.

The book’s takeaways and life lessons are:

• Successful product design and aesthetics
• The importance of having a clear vision and being able to express it to others
• The power of creativity and original thought
• The value of persistence and the ability to rebound from setbacks
• The need to always learn about and adapt to new technologies and fashion trends
• The importance of being around brilliant, enthusiastic people who share your vision Promoting collaboration and teamwork.

CHAPTER XXXVI

"Elon Musk: Tesla, SpaceX, and the Quest for a Fantastic Future." by Ashlee Vance

Elon Musk's life and career are chronicled in Ashlee Vance's biography. Musk's early life in South Africa, his move to the US for college, and his early Silicon Valley career as the founder and CEO of Zip2, PayPal, SpaceX, Tesla, and SolarCity are covered in the book.

Musk's ambitious plans to change energy, space, and transportation are detailed in the book. It also discusses his intense work ethic, desire for success, and marital history and divorces.

The book emphasises Musk's dedication to invention and willingness to take risks to achieve his goals. It also praises his work ethic and creativity.

The book also highlights Musk's tendency to be a demanding boss, argue with employees, and make lofty promises that don't always come true.

The book gives readers a look inside Musk's mind and his strategies for success in various industries.

The book's takeaways and life lessons are:

- Believe in your objective and work hard to achieve it despite obstacles and doubters.
- Take calculated risks and learn from your successes and failures.
- Challenge the status quo and innovate in all areas of your

career.

- Work hard and inspire others.
- Don't be afraid to break the rules.
- Use technology to achieve your aims.
- Stay flexible and focused on the greater picture.
- Work with others who share your values and aspirations.
- Stick to your principles and act decisively when needed.

CHAPTER XXXVII

"The Last Shot: The Story of Michael Jordan's Comeback" by Mark Vancil.

According to "The Last Shot," Michael Jordan returned to basketball in the late 1990s after playing baseball. The book begins with an overview of the Chicago Bulls and NBA, setting the stage for Jordan's return. Mark Vancil examines Jordan's gambling and father's death when he's away from the game.

Michael Jordan's tough training and conditioning to rebound is examined in the book. Jordan's colleagues and Bulls coach Phil Jackson are also examined. The book details Jordan's final NBA season, the 1997–1998 Bulls.

Jordan's impact on basketball and culture is examined throughout the book. He describes how Jordan's on-court dominance and off-court promotion made the NBA a global sensation. Jordan's impact on the shoe industry, especially the launch of his Air Jordan brand, is also covered in the book.

The author concludes Jordan's comeback was effective on and off the court. It showed Jordan's competitiveness and impact on sports, culture, and business.

The book's takeaways and life lessons are:

- The importance of tenacity and willpower in achieving success
- The importance of setting and pursuing goals
- The ability to overcome obstacles and personal issues

- The effectiveness of a solid work ethic and persistence
- The effect of having a successful attitude and mindset
- The importance of having a clear vision and strategy for success
- The value of effective leadership and collaboration

CHAPTER XXXVIII

“Benjamin Franklin: An American Life” by Walter Isaacson

Polymath Benjamin Franklin founded the US. "Benjamin Franklin: An American Life" was written by Walter Isaacson. This Benjamin Franklin biography covers his entire life, from his 1706 birth in Boston through his 1790 death in Philadelphia. This book covers Benjamin Franklin’s writing, inventing, and science. It discusses his political career, including his involvement in the American Revolution and as the first US Ambassador to France. Franklin was a lifelong learner and reader, always seeking new knowledge and methods to improve. He believed that everyone who worked hard to improve might succeed in all aspects of life. Franklin stressed tenacity and hard work. Franklin struggled, yet he never gave up on his ambitions and exploited his failures to improve. The book also shows Franklin’s ability to communicate with people from diverse backgrounds and unite them for a common goal. He excelled at diplomacy and networking throughout his political and diplomatic career. Mastered both. "Benjamin Franklin: An American Life" is a detailed and informative biography of one of the most influential figures in US history. It emphasises timeless values like self-improvement, hard work, perseverance, and connection.

The book’s takeaways and life lessons are:

- Self-educate and keep learning. Benjamin Franklin read a lot and taught himself several skills.
- Franklin's frugality and money management helped him become financially independent. Frugality and budgeting will help you emulate Franklin.
- Benjamin Franklin's greatest achievements came from his desire to try new things and experiment.
- Build lasting ties: Benjamin Franklin was an outstanding connector who built many beneficial professional and personal partnerships that helped him in his economic and political undertakings.
- Prioritize personal development. Benjamin Franklin thought that personal and professional success required intellectual and moral development.

CHAPTER XXXIX

“My Experiments with Truth” by Mahatma Gandhi.

"My Experiments with Truth" is Mahatma Gandhi’s autobiography. The book recounts Gandhi’s childhood and adulthood, including his travels and life lessons. It shows his non-violent struggle and civil disobedience to free India from British rule. The book emphasises Gandhi’s struggle for India’s independence from Britain.

Gandhi emphasises truth and self-awareness throughout the text. He tells how his spiritual path taught him the power of non-violence and helped him win Indian freedom. He describes how he exploited this understanding to win Indian freedom. He also recounts his non-violent fight to inequality and injustice in South Africa, where he spent a large part of his childhood.

The book stresses the importance of self-awareness and self-reflection. Gandhi wrote that he experimented with several beliefs and lifestyles before finding his calling. He invites readers to be open-minded and question their beliefs to find their own path in life.

Another guideline is non-violence. Gandhi shows how peaceful resistance can achieve political, societal, and personal goals. He emphasises self-discipline and persistence as he recounts how he and his followers endured jail time, violence, and other hardships to gain independence.

"My Experiments with Truth" shines a light on one of the 20th century’s most influential political personalities. It highlights the power of self-awareness, nonviolence, and patience.

The book's takeaways and life lessons are:

- Truth and nonviolence underpin all morality.
- Spiritual growth involves self-discipline and self-purification.
- Selfless service to others is the first step to self-realization and completion.
- Civil disobedience can transform society, but only as a last choice.
- A person's inner state matters more than their external circumstances or possessions.
- Meditation and reflection are the only ways to evolve and discover one's purpose.

CHAPTER XL

"Essentialism: The Disciplined Pursuit of Less" by Greg McKeown

"Essentialism: The Disciplined Pursuit of Less," Greg McKeown's productivity book, discusses essentialism, which emphasises life's essentials over its non-essentials. This book provides practical tips for prioritising and letting go of less important things.

The book argues that little is more. McKeown says most people attempt to accomplish too much and take on too many obligations, which causes stress and burnout. He advises readers to learn to prioritise by eliminating non-essential tasks. Readers should also practise focusing on what important.

Extreme ownership is another guideline. McKeown advises his readers to take full responsibility for their life rather than blaming others. He encourages active decision-making and time management.

The book emphasises defining values and determining priorities. McKeown advises readers to decide based on their life goals. He invites readers to consider their life trade-offs and make values-based decisions.

McKeown also recommends "essentialism in the wild." He claims essentialism is both personal and professional. He advises readers to apply essentialism to their jobs by focusing on what matters most.

Finally, McKeown emphasises self-improvement and constant learning. He tells readers to always be open to new ideas.

"Essentialism: The Disciplined Pursuit of Less" encourages readers to focus on what is truly important, take control of their time and energy, and deliberately choose solutions that align with their values. It also encourages readers to use essentialist ideas and stay teachable.

The book's takeaways and life lessons are:

- To focus on what's important, you need to know what's not.
- Prioritize goals based on your values and purpose.
- Learn to reject distractions.
- Eliminate duties and activities that don't support your long-term goals.
- Focusing on streamlining and organising your everyday routine can improve your clarity and efficiency.
- To stay focused and energised, prioritise self-care and relaxation.
- Determine the relevance of each activity or commitment in your life and confirm that it matches your top priorities.
- Realize that success comes from doing the right things, not more.
- Realize that true success involves both attaining your goals and becoming the person you want to be.
- Staying focused, avoiding distractions, and refusing temptations require self-control and discipline.
- Short-term sacrifices are necessary to achieve long-term success and fulfilment.
- Remember that less is more and that simplifying your life and focusing on what matters can help you achieve more and live a more meaningful life. Remember this to maximise your life.

CHAPTER XLI

"Effortless: Make It Easier to Do What Matters Most" by Greg McKeown

Greg McKeown's book "Effortless: Make It Easier to Do What Matters Most" discusses reducing one's life to focus on what matters most. The author claims that distractions and unnecessary work keep us from accomplishing our goals and living a fulfilled life. He advocates prioritising and eliminating non-essentials to make place for what matters most.

The author emphasises several basic principles, including "essentialism." This involves choosing one's most important goals and putting all one's attention, time, and resources towards them. According to the author, this is the key to happiness and success. He also emphasises setting boundaries and knowing how to say no to unnecessary activities and distractions.

The author emphasises mindfulness and self-awareness. He suggests that paying attention to our thoughts and feelings might help us identify what matters most and make better time and energy decisions. Paying attention to our ideas and feelings helps. He also recommends self-reflection to help us understand ourselves and our values.

The author emphasises simplifying surroundings. He advises people to tidy their homes and workplaces to make them more tranquil and focused. Streamlining our stuff and decluttering our homes can also help us focus on what matters.

"Effortless: Make It Easier to Do What Matters Most"

invites readers to simplify their lives to focus on what matters most. The author emphasises essentialism, mindfulness, self-awareness, and simplification to attain success and happiness.

The book's takeaways and life lessons are:

• Prioritize and eliminate activities.
• Prioritize and eliminate unnecessary tasks.
• Break enormous goals into smaller, doable actions.
• Create a "must, should, and desire" framework for decision-making.
• Learn to say no.
• Develop self-awareness to identify and regulate your non-essential tendencies.
• Think "less but better" when allocating time, energy, and resources.
• Review and adapt progress to create a continuous improvement approach. Create a continual improvement system with this.

CHAPTER XLII

"The 80/20 Principle: The Secret to Achieving More with Less" by Richard Koch.

"The 80/20 Principle: The Secret to Achieving More with Less" by Richard Koch discusses the Pareto Principle, sometimes known as the 80/20 rule. This book discusses the Pareto Principle. The book discusses how the 80% rule applies to business, relationships, and personal development. The author suggests focusing on the 20% of goals that matter most to achieve more in less time and with less effort.

This book's chapters explore the Pareto Principle and how it can be used to achieve goals. The book uses real-life examples and case studies to illustrate its principles. He also gives the reader challenges and suggestions for using the 80/20 principle to their own lives.

This book emphasises the need of focusing on the vital few rather than the insignificant many. The author claims that by identifying the 20% of activities that matter, one may achieve more with less effort and better results. He also emphasises setting priorities and focusing on what counts rather to getting bogged down by unimportant tasks.

Leverage is another key concept explained in the literature. The author shows that focusing on the 20% of one's tasks that matter can quadruple one's efforts and improve results. He also emphasises delegating and outsourcing non-essential tasks to free up time and energy for more important tasks.

"The 80/20 Principle: The Secret to Achieving More with Less" provides a practical, actionable approach for achieving more with less work. It offers readers practical guidance and activities to apply the 80/20 principle to their life and a fresh perspective on how to identify and prioritise their priorities.

The book's takeaways and life lessons are:

• Focusing on the few tasks that will yield the most returns.
• Applying the 80/20 rule to gain time, money, and energy.
• Use the 80/20 rule to uncover the root cause of a problem and find the best solution.
• The 80/20 rule can help one choose the best alternative.
• Using the 80/20 rule to prioritise important relationships in personal and professional life.
• Understanding the importance of the 80/20 rule in business and how it may increase productivity, effectiveness, and income
• Realizing that the 80/20 rule applies to many facets of life, such as health, relationships, and personal development, and applying it to improve them.

CHAPTER XLIII

"The Miracle Morning: The Not-So-Obvious Secret Guaranteed to Transform Your Life" by Hal Elrod.

Hal Elrod's self-help book "The Miracle Morning" emphasises the power of morning rituals to improve one's life. The book recommends six daily "Miracle Morning" activities. The "Miracle Morning" routine. Practices include:
-Silent meditation or prayer
-Affirmations
-Visualization
-Exercise
-Reading
-Scribing
The book's author claims that adding certain morning habits can boost productivity, happiness, and quality of life. The book also offers actionable advice for creating and maintaining a morning routine and personal stories from people whose lives have improved after implementing the Miracle Morning.
The book argues that while we all have 24 hours a day, how we use them determines our quality of life. If we spend the first hour of each day on self-development, we may be more successful and get more done. The book emphasises the importance of a consistent, disciplined morning routine and encourages readers to be patient and persistent.
"S.A.V.E.R.S."—silence, affirmation, visualisation, exercise, reading, and scribing—can also be used. This acronym

represents the principle's principles. To focus and energise your mind, body, and spirit, do it in the morning or evening.

In conclusion, The Miracle Morning advises readers to have an open mind and try various techniques because the regimen may not work for everyone. It encourages readers to experiment and find their best technique.

The book's takeaways and life lessons are:

- Silence: Starting your day with silence, followed by meditation or prayer, will help you focus on what's important.
- Affirmations: Chanting positive affirmations can help you stay positive and focused on your goals.
- Visualization: seeing yourself having achieved your goals and being the person you want to be helps you feel like you can achieve them.
- Exercise: Starting the day with any physical activity will boost your attitude and energy.
- Reading: starting the day with a book that inspires or enlightens you can set the tone for the day.
- Write your Thoughts, Goal and Plans: Writing out your goals and intentions can clarify and make them more actionable.

CHAPTER XLIV

“High Performance Habits: How Extraordinary People Become That Way” by Brendon Burchard.

"High Performance Habits: How Extraordinary People Become That Way" by self-help author Brendon Burchard aims to teach readers the habits needed for success in any field.

Burchard’s book highlights the six behaviours he believes are important to realise one’s full potential and perform well. Clarity, energy, productivity, influence, courage, and raising the bar are these habits. He also provides a full guide on how to implement these practises.

Burchard emphasises self-awareness throughout the text. He encourages readers to examine their thoughts, feelings, and actions to identify their strengths and weaknesses. He also emphasises the importance of clearly stating one’s goals and establishing a sense of urgency.

Burchard also emphasises optimising physical and emotional vitality. He recommends readers to control their emotional well-being by practising mindfulness and positive thinking, and their physical health by exercising, getting enough sleep, and eating well.

Burchard also emphasises building relationships and growing one’s impact. He advises readers to develop leadership and communication skills to influence others. He also recommends building a positive support system.

Finally, Burchard emphasises bravery and following one’s ideas. He urges readers to overcome fear and take risks to achieve their goals. He also teaches ways to overcome obstacles and flourish.

"High Performance Habits" will help readers improve in every area of their lives. The literature emphasises self-awareness, goals, positive habits, connections, and action. It gives readers the skills and strategies to perform well and reach their potential.

The book's takeaways and life lessons are:

• "Seeking clarity" is being clear about what you want, why you want it, and how you'll acquire it.

• "Generating energy" is maintaining one's physical, emotional, mental, and spiritual health to maintain energy and attention.

• "Raising necessity" is fostering urgency and determination to achieve goals.

• Focusing on the most critical tasks and efficiently managing time and resources increases productivity.

• Building relationships and communicating well are habits that build influence.

•Courage is taking risks despite fear and uncertainty.

CHAPTER XLV

"Finish What You Start: The Art of Following Through, Taking Action, Executing, & Self-Discipline" by Jan Yager.

Jan Yager's self-help book "Finish What You Start" teaches readers how to focus and finish their goals. Chapters cover different aspects of following through. Set goals, create a strategy, overcome obstacles, and stay motivated.

Throughout the book, setting clear and explicit goals is stressed. This involves identifying your goal, breaking it down into manageable chunks, and creating a plan of action that details the steps you need to take to achieve it.

Acting is another crucial concept. The author stresses throughout the book that you must keep going despite obstacles. This requires a lot of self-discipline and tenacity.

The book also emphasises focusing on one task at a time rather than trying to finish too many at once. This reduces distractions and boosts productivity.

The author also suggests using a daily reminder system to stay on track and focused on your goals and keeping a progress journal to stay motivated and track your success.

"Finish What You Start" is a guide that helps readers focus, discipline, and finish their projects.

The book's takeaways and life lessons are:

- Set clear, detailed goals and break them down into manageable tasks.

Prioritize the most important tasks.

• Take ownership of your actions and decisions.

• Create a schedule and stick to it to avoid procrastination and distractions.

• Always choose solutions that align with your long-term goals and values.

• Learn from mistakes and use them to improve.

• Visualization and positive affirmations can help you achieve your goals.

• Find mentors or accountability partners to help you achieve your life goals.

CHAPTER XLVI

“Organize Tomorrow Today: 8 Ways to Retrain Your Mind to Optimize Performance at Work and in Life” by Dr. Jason Selk, Tom Bartow,

"Organize Tomorrow Today: 8 Ways to Retrain Your Mind to Optimize Performance at Work and in Life" is a self-help book by Dr. Jason Selk, Tom Bartow, and Matthew Rudy. The book is designed to help individuals improve their performance at work and in life by retraining their minds to be more focused, productive, and effective. The book is divided into three parts.

In the first part, the authors introduce the concept of mental toughness, which involves training your mind to be more disciplined, focused, and resilient. They explain the importance of mental toughness for success in both personal and professional life.

In the second part, the authors present their "8 Ways" system, which provides practical strategies for retraining your mind to optimize performance. These strategies include setting goals, creating a daily plan, developing a positive mindset, using visualization techniques, and focusing on key priorities.

In the third part, the authors show how to apply these strategies to different areas of life, including work, relationships, health, and personal growth. They provide real-world examples and case studies to demonstrate how these strategies can be used to achieve greater success and fulfillment.

Overall, "Organize Tomorrow Today" offers a comprehensive approach to improving performance and achieving success in all areas of life. The book provides practical strategies for retraining your mind to be more disciplined, focused, and effective, and demonstrates how these strategies can be applied to achieve greater success and fulfillment.

The book's takeaways and life lessons are:

• Mental toughness is the key to achieving success and fulfillment in personal and professional life.
• The "8 Ways" system provides practical strategies for retraining your mind to optimize performance, including setting goals, creating a daily plan, developing a positive mindset, using visualization techniques, and focusing on key priorities.
• Consistency and discipline are essential for achieving long-term success and reaching your goals.
• Mental toughness is not just about being physically tough or competitive, but also about being mentally strong and resilient.
• A positive mindset is a key component of mental toughness, and can be developed through daily affirmations and positive self-talk.
• Visualization techniques can be used to enhance performance by mentally rehearsing successful outcomes.
• It is important to identify and focus on key priorities in order to achieve greater success and fulfillment.
• The strategies presented in the book can be applied to all areas of life, including work, relationships, health, and personal growth.

CHAPTER XLVII

“The New One Minute Manager” by Ken Blanchard and Spencer Johnson

"The New One Minute Manager" by Ken Blanchard and Spencer Johnson is a management classic. The book claims that three basic management tactics can be implemented in one minute to achieve efficient management. Any order works for the techniques.

Setting Employee Goals The first technique emphasises setting clear, quantifiable goals for employees and working with them to create action plans to attain them. This technique helps people take responsibility of their job and understand their roles and responsibilities.

Gratitude Rewarding staff for good work is the second technique. One-minute praises. Consistent praise and feedback, according to the authors, keeps workers motivated and engaged. Positive feedback builds trust and respect, which improves workplace performance and productivity.

The third technique, "One Minute Reprimands," addresses performance difficulties quickly and effectively. The authors believe that addressing concerns immediately reduces their negative effects on the organisation. Managers may foster accountability and responsibility by setting clear expectations and providing feedback.

The book is easy to read and offers practical advice on how to apply these tactics in real life. This post is for managers who want to improve their management skills and build a more productive team.

The book's takeaways and life lessons are:

• The One Minute Manager emphasises "caught people doing something right" and applauding them. This method builds trust and goodwill between managers and employees.
• The literature emphasises setting clear, quantifiable goals for oneself and one's team. This ensures that everyone has the same goals and understands them.
•Active listening and communication are also crucial to effective management, according to the authors. Managers should regularly check in with their workers, solicit feedback, and handle any issues.
• The book also emphasises informal and continuous staff connections.
• The New One Minute Manager emphasises the need of delegating work and tasks throughout its material. This helps employees grow their skills and confidence while freeing up management time.
• The book promotes rewarding and recognising employees who exceed goals. • Finally, the book advises managers to be adaptable and open to new ways of doing things. Managers stay current with this mindset.

CHAPTER XLVIII

"Do It Today: Master Productivity, Discipline, and Focus" by Darius Foroux.

"Do It Today: Master Productivity, Discipline, and Focus" by Darius Foroux helps readers become more productive, disciplined, and focused to achieve their goals and live a more rewarding life. Three main sections—Productivity, Discipline, and Focus—make up the book.

The first section, "Productivity," explains that working smarter, not harder, increases productivity. He lists some ways to boost productivity:

Prioritizing tasks: picking the most important ones and doing them first.

Distractions are anything that distracts you from your task.

Goal-setting: Having a defined goal and approach.

The second section, "Discipline," discusses how self-discipline helps us achieve our goals. He suggests the following ways to develop discipline:

To achieve your goals, you must create a routine.

Staying accountable involves monitoring your progress and holding others accountable.

Habits help you achieve goals.

"Focus," the third and final portion, illustrates why being focused is essential to achieving our goals. He suggests several ways to focus:

Distractions are anything that distracts you from your task.

Clear goals require a plan to achieve them.

Prioritize your chores by focusing on the most critical ones.

The book's takeaways and life lessons are:

• defining and prioritising goals to stay focused and motivated.
• Breaking complex activities into smaller, more manageable segments increases productivity.
• Goal-setting and self-accountability require deadlines.
• developing self-control and discipline to meet obligations.
• Avoiding distractions and unimportant chores
• Regularly reviewing and changing practises to increase efficiency and effectiveness.

CHAPTER XLIX

"The Heart to Start: Win the Inner War and Let Your Art Shine" by David Kadavy.

"The Heart to Start" by David Kadavy covers the inner struggles and insecurities that sometimes limit creative people from following their passions and sharing their work. The author explores the psychological reasons people procrastinate and don't follow through on their ideas and offers solutions.

The book's main concept, "heartstarting," involves deliberately confronting and conquering the anxieties and doubts that impede one from starting a project. The author recommends readers to identify their individual anxieties, such as failure or rejection, and take active actions to overcome them to continue their pursuits.

The book emphasises consistency and perseverance. In every field, but especially in the arts, Kadavy stresses the significance of sustained work throughout time. He advises setting small, achievable goals and working steadily towards them instead of focusing on huge goals.

The author also emphasises self-reflection and introspection as essential to creativity. He advises readers to explore their motives, objectives, and beliefs to create true, meaningful work.

In conclusion, "The Heart to Start" gives creatives practical ways to overcome internal obstacles. It also stimulates self-reflection, constant effort, and facing fears to attain goals.

The book's takeaways and life lessons are:

• Recognizing and being aware of the mental obstacles that prevent you from starting and finishing creative projects
• Engaging in self-awareness practises to understand one's own creative process • Developing a "beginner's mindset" to approach new projects with openness and curiosity
• Using strategies like "time-blocking" to schedule specific and allotted time to work on your assignments
• A strong support network will help you stay motivated and accountable while pursuing your goals.
• Creating a "success ritual" to help you focus and get "in the zone" before work • Dividing large undertakings into smaller subtasks to make them seem less overwhelming
• "The Pomodoro Technique" improves time management and productivity.

CHAPTER L

“The One Thing: The Surprisingly Simple Truth Behind Extraordinary Results” by Gary Keller and Jay Papasan.

Gary Keller and Jay Papasan’s book "The One Thing" explores the idea that focusing on the most important thing in life can lead to great results. If they avoid distractions and focus on one task, people can achieve more than they thought possible, according to the authors.

This book provides a framework for identifying and prioritising "the one thing" in one’s career, health, and relationships. It also offers strategies for overcoming procrastination, distractions, and staying motivated.

"The Focusing Question" is one of the book’s most valuable lessons. This question helps people identify their "one thing" in any area of life. "What is the one thing I can do to make everything else easy or unnecessary?"

"The Four Thieves of Productivity"—interruptions, distractions, multitasking, and the environment—is another key concept. The book encourages readers to identify and eliminate time wasters to be productive and focused.

The text also emphasises action and drive. The authors believe that starting with simple tasks and progressively increasing their difficulty can help people overcome their fear and reluctance and achieve their goals.

Finally, the author emphasises the importance of a daily routine that emphasises the "one thing" and promotes concentration and production. This includes setting up a productive workspace and scheduling time to work on specific projects.

The book's takeaways and life lessons are:

• choosing the "one item" needed to achieve a goal and focusing all efforts, energy, and attention on it
• Eliminating time-wasters to focus on the "one thing" that matters.
• Setting a "big, hairy, audacious goal" (BHAG) that is challenging and motivating helps one keep focused and motivated.
• Asking the "Focusing Question"—"What's the ONE Thing I can accomplish so that by doing it everything else will be easier or unnecessary?"—may help one decide which activity or goal is most important.
• creating a "domino effect" by identifying the most important action or goal and then breaking it down into doable subtasks that nevertheless achieve the main goal.
• Recognizing the importance of discipline and consistency to stay focused on "the one thing" and reach one's goal.
• Taking action and "getting started" on the "one thing" is stressed over planning or overthinking.
• Striking a good balance and taking care of oneself is essential to long-term concentration and productivity.

CHAPTER LI

“Hyperfocus: How to work less and achieve more” is a book written by Chris Bailey

"Hyperfocus: How to Work Less and Achieve More" by Chris Bailey. This book explains hyperfocus, a state of intense attention and productivity, and how to apply it. The author shares his personal experiences, research, and tips for achieving hyperfocus in your personal and professional life.

The book emphasises the importance of setting clear and explicit goals. Without clear goals, it's hard to focus and stay motivated, the author says. SMARTER goals—Specific, Measurable, Achievable, Relevant, Time-bound, and Evaluated—are his recommendation.

The book emphasises the importance of minimising distractions. Disabling notifications and creating a private workspace are among the author's suggestions for achieving hyperfocus.

The book also discusses how mindfulness and pauses can improve focus and productivity. The author recommends the Pomodoro Technique, which involves working for 25 minutes and taking a 5-minute break.

The book also discusses productivity's role in creating a sense of purpose and direction in one's work and life. Instead of working harder, the author suggests working smarter and more efficiently to get more done in less time and have more time for our hobbies.

"Hyperfocus: How to work less and achieve more" provides

tips for focusing and being productive. Establishing clear goals, minimising distractions, taking breaks, practising mindfulness, and having a sense of purpose and direction in one's personal and professional life can help.

The book's takeaways and life lessons are:

- Focus on your most important tasks.
- Reset your body and mind regularly.
- Disabling notifications and creating a workspace can reduce interruptions.
- Use the Pomodoro technique to break your task into short, focused chunks.
- To maintain a healthy work-life balance, set clear boundaries.
- See which productivity methods work best for you.
- Mindfulness and self-awareness help you manage your mental condition.
- Accept "good enough" instead of striving for perfection.
- Decline non-essential engagements and chores to make time for what's important.
- Assessing and revising your productivity strategy regularly might help you reach your goals.

CHAPTER LII

“The 7 Habits of Highly Effective People: Powerful Lessons in Personal Change” by Stephen Covey

"The 7 Habits of Highly Effective People" by Stephen Covey explores the principles and habits that successful people use to achieve their goals and live a fulfilling life. Three sections—"Private Victory," "Public Victory," and "Paradigms and Principles"—make up the book.

In the first section, "Paradigms and Principles," Covey introduces "paradigm shift." This term describes changing one’s mindset and worldview. He thinks that successful people have a different worldview than unsuccessful people, and the first step to achieving one’s goals is changing one’s perspective on how to get there.

The second segment, "Private Victory," emphasises self-improvement exercises. Be proactive, start with the end in mind, prioritise, think win-win, and first comprehend, then be understood. Covey advises mastering these behaviours to feel in control and peaceful.

In the final section, "Public Victory," Covey discusses interpersonal and collaborative success behaviours. These include synergizing, polishing one’s saw, finding one’s voice, and helping others find theirs. He says these practises are vital for building strong personal and professional connections and creating an environment where everyone can thrive.

Stephen R. Covey uses real-life stories and examples to demonstrate his concepts and practises. He also gives readers assignments and advice to help them adopt these practises.

The book's takeaways and life lessons are:

• Being proactive involves taking charge and owning one's actions and decisions.
• Starting with the end in mind involves setting clear, specific goals and picturing how to achieve them.
• Putting first things first means prioritising other tasks and managing time.
• Thinking in a way that serves both sides means finding solutions that benefit both parties and taking satisfaction in others‘ successes.
• "Seeking first to understand, then to be understood" means listening to others and trying to see things from their perspective.
• Synergizing means collaborating to achieve goals.
"Sharpening the saw" requires good physical, mental, emotional, and spiritual health.
• Finding your voice, helping others find theirs, communicating well, and appreciating others' differences.

CHAPTER LIII

“Eat That Frog!: 21 Great Ways to Stop Procrastinating and Get More Done in Less Time” by Brian Tracy.

"Eat That Frog!" was written by productivity expert Brian Tracy. It has 21 ways to beat procrastination and get more done faster. The book’s idea is that if you start each day by "eating the frog," which is shorthand for accomplishing the hardest or most time-consuming task, you will be more effective and productive.

Procrastination’s psychology and causes are examined in the book’s first section. After that, Tracy offers strategies for beating procrastination and increasing productivity. One of his most important tips is to set clear, defined goals and then break them down into smaller, more manageable tasks. He also suggests using a time management strategy like the Pomodoro technique to stay focused and avoid distractions.

Tracy’s book also teaches how to say "no" to unimportant things, delegate tasks, and use positive self-talk to overcome limiting beliefs. In order to boost productivity, the author advises readers to exercise, eat right, and get enough sleep.

Throughout the book, Tracy provides real-life examples and case studies of people who have successfully implemented the tactics. Throughout the book are these examples and case studies. "21 Great Ways to Stop Procrastinating" is a quick reference guide at the book’s end.

Setting clear and specific goals, breaking down tasks into smaller and more manageable steps, using time management techniques, learning to say "no" to unimportant tasks, delegating tasks to others, using positive self-talk to overcome limiting beliefs, taking care of one's physical and emotional well-being, and using real-life examples and case studies for inspiration are some of the principles from this book that can be implemented.

The book's takeaways and life lessons are:

• Finish the most crucial task first. This strategy is called "eating the frog."
• Break big tasks into smaller, manageable steps.
• Prioritize and schedule tasks.
• Use the "80/20 rule" to prioritise high-value tasks.
• Eliminate distractions and improve time management.
• Learn to say no.
Regular practise builds self-discipline and responsibility.
• Focus on the current task.
• Encourage yourself and visualise to overcome procrastination.
• Monitoring and analysing your progress will help you improve.

CHAPTER LIV

“The 4-Hour Work Week” by Timothy Ferriss.

The best-selling personal development book "The 4-Hour Work Week" by Timothy Ferriss shows readers how to work less and achieve more success and freedom. Four sections—"Definition," "Elimination," "Automation," and "Liberation"—make up the book.

Ferriss introduces the "New Rich" (NR) concept here. Lifestyle design and automation help the NR achieve their goals and live their own lives. He also discusses identifying and eliminating non-essential activities.

Elimination: How to identify and eliminate activities that aren’t necessary for success but are holding you back. It shows how to use the "80/20 rule" to prioritise and organise your work.

Automation: Ferriss shows how to automate your revenue streams and other aspects of your life, such as reducing your workload with technology and outsourcing.

This section discusses how to achieve your goals by breaking free from traditional labour and living your dream life. It will teach you how to create a "muse," or passive income business, travel and live abroad, and live an exciting, independent life.

Ferriss encourages readers to challenge their beliefs about work and success and take control of their lives by trying different lifestyle and business models. He also challenges work and success beliefs. He also emphasises taking action rather than just daydreaming.

The book's takeaways and life lessons are:

• "DEAL" to efficiently eliminate tasks and delegate responsibility.
• The "low-information diet" reduces distractions and boosts focus.
• The "Pareto Principle" suggests focusing on the 20% of actions that provide 80% of results.
• The "80/20" principle helps identify and prioritise career and personal priorities.
• The "E-Myth" can help business owners distinguish between working on and working in their companies.
• The "minimum feasible lifestyle" is obtaining one's ideal lifestyle while minimising expenses and maximising revenue.
• The "muse" for creating a business that generates passive money and gives the owner more freedom and flexibility is a business that can be run without the owner's input.
• The "four-hour weekday" balances money, lifestyle, and happiness.

CHAPTER LV

"What They Don't Teach You at Harvard Business School: Notes from a Street-Smart Executive" by Mark H. McCormack.

Mark H. McCormack wrote "What They Don't Teach You at Harvard Business School" as a businessman and sports marketing pioneer. This book gives tangible advice for succeeding in a competitive business climate based on the author's professional and personal experiences.

The book emphasises the importance of building relationships. McCormack stresses the importance of networking and capitalising on those contacts to advance one's profession. He also emphasises the need of being proactive in one's career rather than waiting for opportunities.

The novel also emphasises perseverance. In this book, McCormack uses experiences from his own life to encourage readers to keep trying despite setbacks. He also stresses the importance of being flexible and receptive to new ideas in the corporate environment.

The book also emphasises professional self-confidence and aggressiveness. McCormack advises readers to speak up and take charge of their careers rather than waiting for others to decide.

The book is mostly about McCormack's corporate success advice. Negotiation, time management, and clear communication are examples. He also shares his personal experiences and career lessons, providing a unique

perspective on business.
"What They Don't Teach You at Harvard Business School" provides practical business advice. The author emphasises networking, persistence, adaptability, confidence, and aggressiveness. This book is a wonderful resource for businesspeople because the author draws on his personal experiences and career lessons.

The book's takeaways and life lessons are:

•The power of being able to make quick decisions based on accurate information
• The importance of being flexible and open to new experiences and perspectives
• The value of surrounding oneself with a capable group of advisors and mentors to provide support and guidance
•The importance of being aware of and using leverage in various settings; the usefulness of having a transparent awareness of one's own capabilities and limitations; and the importance of maintaining a high level of discipline, attention, and work ethic.

CHAPTER LVI

"The Side Hustle: From Idea to Income in 27 Days" by Chris Guillebeau.

Author and entrepreneur Chris Guillebeau wrote "The Side Hustle: From Idea to Income in 27 Days." NYT Bestselling Author published this book. This book shows you how to start a profitable side business in a month. Idea Generation, Testing and Validation, and Launch and Scale make up the book.

"Idea Generation" in this guide helps users create a side business plan. It covers finding the perfect opportunity, understanding your unique abilities and passions, and finding market gaps. Guillebeau includes exercises to help readers generate and evaluate ideas.

The article's "Testing and Validation" section tests and refines the idea before launch. Guillebeau addresses market research, minimal viable products, and client feedback. He also gives practical activities to help readers validate and revise their views.

"Launch and Scale," the last chapter, covers starting and growing a side business. Guillebeau covers business planning, website building, and side hustle advertising. He also gives readers exercises to establish and build their side company.

Guillebeau gives several real-life side business examples and lessons throughout the book. He urges action and perseverance in the face of adversity. He also emphasises having a clear goal and a plan to achieve it.

The book's takeaways and life lessons are:

- Your side company needs a productive audience.
- Researching the industry and confirming your idea's viability
- Making a customer-friendly offer
- Creating a firm website and online presence
- Using digital platforms, such as social media, to connect with and engage customers
- Building a support system and a network of possible collaborators
- Testing, refining, and improving your side hustle to boost profits

CHAPTER LVII

“Rework” by Jason Fried and David Heinemeier Hansson.

"Rework" writers Basecamp co-founders. Jason Fried and David Heinemeier Hansson wrote the book. This book helps business owners and entrepreneurs build a lucrative, long-term enterprise. The contributors examine leadership, productivity, and marketing from their own experiences and perspectives.

The book promotes the idea that "less is more" throughout. The authors argue that business owners may do more with less work if they simplify and streamline their operations. They also stress the need of taking action and not overthinking.

The book emphasises "scratching your own itch" as well. The authors suggest that successful businesses address demands or solve problems that the founders have faced. Establishing a personal connection to a problem helps entrepreneurs become passionate and devoted to solving it. The reader is advised to focus on their company’s capabilities rather than trying to please everyone. The authors suggest that enterprises focus on their strengths and outsource or subcontract the rest.

The book also emphasises adaptability and flexibility. The writers advise entrepreneurs to be open to new ideas and ready to change direction when necessary.

"Rework" is a practical and easy guide for entrepreneurs and small business owners on how to develop a successful and sustainable firm by reducing processes, focusing on your strengths, and being adaptive. The author wanted to give entrepreneurs and small business owners a simple and useful handbook.

The book's takeaways and life lessons are:

- Launching a minimum viable product (MVP) and iterating depending on consumer feedback rather than a perfect product.
- Being flexible in case a strategy fails.
- emphasising team communication.
- Understanding the need of delegating and letting go to grow a business.
- outsourcing your weaknesses and focusing on your strengths.
- Staying small can prevent overdevelopment.
- Stressing the need of relaxing and recharging.
- building a business around a passion.
- Emphasizing hiring the appropriate people rather than just those with the right qualifications.
- Focus on your target demographic rather than trying to please everyone.
- Emphasizing the importance of preserving one's essential convictions and refusing to compromise them for success

CHAPTER LVIII

"The Hard Thing About Hard Things: Building a Business When There Are No Easy Answers" by Ben Horowitz

Ben Horowitz, a renowned businessman and venture capitalist, wrote "The Hard Thing About Hard Things" in 2014. This book discusses the difficulty of starting and running a business and offers solutions.

The book emphasises the need of being honest with oneself regarding current events. Horowitz emphasises that great leaders must accept and acknowledge the unpleasant facts of operating a business rather than avoiding or sugarcoating them. He thinks this is the only way to succeed.

Another element is the importance of self-awareness and adaptability. Horowitz believes that any business must be able to adapt and innovate.

The book also emphasises the necessity of having a clear vision and strategy for the company's future and communicating that vision to employees and stakeholders. Horowitz also highlights the importance of building a strong team and creating a culture of accountability and ownership in the organisation.

In its concluding chapter, the book examines the need of making difficult decisions and how to handle the emotional and psychological stress of leadership. Horowitz advises on stress management and work-life balance.

The book is a realistic and informative look at real-life company leadership issues and gives significant lessons and insights on how to overcome them.

The book's takeaways and life lessons are:

• Accept the struggle: Horowitz advises realising that creating a business is hard and will present numerous obstacles. He tells readers to embrace the challenge and learn from it.
• Lead from the front: In times of uncertainty and disaster, Horowitz emphasises leadership. He encourages leaders to take charge and create an example for the team.
• Communicate well: Horowitz stresses the importance of good communication in corporate development. He recommends executives to communicate openly and honestly with employees, clients, and partners.
•Horowitz urges you to empower your staff to make decisions and act. He advises leaders to give their teams autonomy and resources to succeed.
• Learn from your mistakes: Horowitz emphasises learning from mistakes and improving. He advises executives to take risks, fail, and use their mistakes to better their decision-making.
• Prioritize what matters most: Horowitz tells readers to put the most important things in their lives first. He stresses the need of setting clear goals, creating a strategy, and focusing on what matters most.
• Horowitz emphasises staying calm in difficult situations. He advises leaders to stay calm and make rational decisions.

CHAPTER LIX

"The 1-Page Marketing Plan: Get New Customers, Make More Money, And Stand Out From The Crowd" by Allan Dib.

Allan Dib's "The 1-Page Marketing Plan" can help entrepreneurs and small business owners increase sales and customers. The book emphasises keeping marketing strategies simple and focused. The book's main thesis is that a good marketing strategy can be reduced to one page, making it easy to understand and implement.

The author emphasises the importance of understanding the target market and the business's value to it. He then presents a one-page marketing strategy development process. Determine the unique selling proposition, set goals and objectives, and outline the budget.

The book covers search engine optimization, social media marketing, email marketing, content creation, and plan evaluation.

The book emphasises testing and experimentation in marketing. The author advises readers to monitor and adjust their marketing efforts as needed.

The book also discusses how to stand out in today's oversaturated market. The author emphasises the importance of differentiating a company from its competitors by focusing on its unique selling proposition and brand identity.

"The 1-Page Marketing Plan" is a simple guide for small business owners looking to increase sales and customers.

The book's principles can be easily applied by any company trying to boost its marketing.

The book's takeaways and life lessons are:

• Determine your USP and market.
• Understand the purchase process and create a marketing message for each stage.
• Tailor your product, pricing, locale, and promotion to your USP and target market.
• Data simplifies marketing success tracking.
•Testing and refining your marketing plan improves results.
•Create a one-page paper that clearly explains your marketing approach and goals.
•Direct response marketing simplifies client action.
•Use the internet and digital marketing to spread your message.
• Connect with influential people and businesses to increase your reach and credibility.
• Focus and stay on track when implementing your marketing plan.

CHAPTER LX

“The $100 Startup: Reinvent the Way You Make a Living, Do What You Love, and Create a New Future” by Chris Guillebeau.

"The $100 Startup" by Chris Guillebeau encourages people to turn their passions into profitable businesses. 2013. The book argues that anyone can start a business with little money and resources and provides a step-by-step guide.

The author profiles fifty entrepreneurs who started firms with $100 or less. This book provides practical advice on how to find a winning company idea, validate it with clients, and create a sustainable business plan.

The book emphasises the importance of creating a USP for your organisation. This involves identifying what makes your company unique and emphasising that benefit in your marketing.

Using online platforms and tools to connect with clients saves time and money. Before expanding, the book emphasises refining and testing your business strategy.

The author also emphasises knowing one’s target audience and adapting business practises accordingly. He suggests market research, creating a customer avatar, and identifying the target market’s pain points to create a solution.

"The $100 Startup" can help hobbyists turn their passion into a business. The book discusses finding a unique selling proposition, using online platforms and technologies, testing and iterating your business model, understanding and serving your target market, and market research.

The book's takeaways and life lessons are:

• Finding a USP The book emphasises the importance of finding a unique selling point for your company. This could be a unique product or service, a new take on an established business, or a strong personal brand.
• Putting the client first: the author emphasises knowing one's market and adjusting one's firm to meet its needs throughout the book. This involves understanding their issues and creating solutions.
• Creating an MVP (MVP) The book advises budding entrepreneurs to start small and create a "minimally viable product" (MVP) to test and enhance. This reduces risk and allows experimentation and learning.
• This book advises aspiring entrepreneurs to use existing resources to start a business. Existing resources include networks, abilities, and equipment.
• Diversifying income sources: This book urges business owners to investigate many ways to vary their income and create multiple revenue streams.
• Learning from failure The book teaches business owners to take risks and learn from failure.

CHAPTER LXI

“Good to Great: Why Some Companies Make the Leap... and Others Don't” by Jim Collins.

"Good to Great: Why Some Companies Make the Leap... and Others Don’t" by Jim Collins explains why some businesses succeed and others fail. Collins and his team researched what makes great companies great in this book. The book describes several important discoveries and guiding principles that businesses can use to improve performance and success.

The book emphasises the importance of a clear and appealing vision for the organisation. The study found that businesses with clear goals were the most successful.

The book also discusses "Level 5" leaders, who are modest but driven to succeed. The study found that the most successful business owners balance their aspirations with their humility.

The book also emphasises the importance of discipline and focus. The study found that businesses that focused on their main business and avoided diversions were the most successful.

The book concludes with the importance of corporate social responsibility. The study found that successful businesses balanced their desire to make money with their desire to help society and the environment.

"Good to Great" examines the traits and principles that distinguish great companies from good ones. This book’s insightful information and actionable advice will help companies and leaders succeed.

The book's takeaways and life lessons are:

• The Hedgehog Concept: The book's author advises businesses to focus on their strengths and enjoy, avoiding distractions.
• Leadership at Level 5: Collins believes great firms are led by "Level 5" leaders, who are humble but strong. These leaders drive company success. These leaders can balance company and employee needs and make tough decisions.
• The Flywheel Effect: The book advises businesses to build momentum by making small, consistent changes rather than trying to make a big change.
•The Stockdale Paradox argues that successful company executives must trust that their company will succeed in the long run while accepting harsh realities.
• Technology Accelerators: The book's author recommends firms to utilise technology to boost their good-to-great practises, not as a silver bullet.

CHAPTER LXII

“The 22 Immutable Laws of Branding” by Al Ries and Laura Ries.

Laura and Al Ries wrote "The 22 Immutable Laws of Branding." It’s meant to be an all-encompassing brand-building handbook. Based on the authors' extensive marketing and branding experience, the book has 22 chapters on distinct branding elements.

The language emphasises focus throughout. Businesses must focus on one aspect of their operations to build strong brands, according to the authors. They also advise businesses to focus on one group rather than trying to appeal to all. "The Law of the Category" describes this principle.

The book discusses differentiation extensively. In a crowded market, businesses must differentiate themselves from their competitors, according to the writers. Using unique traits, innovative products, or a strong brand identity can achieve this. Leadership’s Law is this idea.

The book also emphasises brand consistency. Businesses must maintain coherence in their words and images to build a strong brand, according to the writers. This includes keeping the brand’s logo, colour scheme, and messaging consistent across all media.

The book also discusses the Law of the Word, which suggests that a brand should have a memorable name, and the Law of the Firm, which states that a brand should be strongly associated with its parent company. The authors also discuss the need of brand management and innovation

CHAPTER LXIII

“The E-Myth Revisited: Why Most Small Businesses Don't Work and What to Do About It” by Michael E. Gerber.

Michael E. Gerber’s "The E-Myth Revisited: Why Most Small Businesses Don’t Work and What to Do About It" examines small business owners' common mistakes. This book claims that many small business owners are "technicians" who are good at their jobs but lack the business and management skills needed to succeed.

Small business owners can use the book’s concepts to improve their chances of success. A "business prototype"—a detailed plan for the company’s operations—is a key tenet. This includes identifying the target market’s demographics, creating a unique selling proposition, and developing a consistent delivery strategy.

Building a solid "business infrastructure"—the people, procedures, and technologies needed to run the company efficiently—is another crucial component. This includes smart employee hires, efficient sales and marketing operations, and a robust financial management structure.

The book also emphasises comprehensive company management. This entails balancing technical, managerial, and entrepreneurial aspects of the organisation. This means small business owners should focus on both their work and the firm.

The book also urges small business owners to learn from their mistakes, try new ideas, and improve their operations.

It also emphasises the need to adapt to market changes to stay competitive.
"The E-Myth Revisited" can help small business owners improve their management skills and increase their company's chances of success. It provides basic advice on building a sound business foundation and adapting to the ever-changing business world.

The book's takeaways and life lessons are:

• Knowing the difference between working on and in your business is crucial.
• Establishing repeatable methods and procedures to create a company that can run without you.
• focusing on the most important duties that move the organisation ahead and outsourcing the rest.
• Recruiting a reliable team that can contribute to corporate operations and assume more responsibility.
• Assessing and improving corporate operations using measurements and KPIs.
• Manage and grow the firm proactively rather than reactively.

CHAPTER LXIV

“The Lean Startup: How Today's Entrepreneurs Use Continuous Innovation to Create Radically Successful Businesses” by Eric Ries.

Eric Ries‘ book "The Lean Startup: How Today’s Entrepreneurs Use Continuous Innovation to Create Radically Successful Businesses" focuses on efficiency and innovation to start and run a successful business. "How Today’s Entrepreneurs Use Continuous Innovation to Create Radically Successful Businesses" describes the method. This book has three sections: Vision, Steer, and Accelerate.

Ries explains the Lean Startup process under "Vision." "Validated learning," "innovation accounting," and "building-measuring-learning feedback loops" are examples. He says that creating a detailed business plan and then implementing it is often a recipe for failure because it doesn’t account for the market’s unpredictability and uncertainty. Instead, he proposes that new businesses should centre their efforts on verified learning, which refers to the process of putting your company hypotheses to the test using data from the actual world as quickly and frequently as you can.

In "Accelerate," Ries discusses scaling a startup. He believes that scaling an enterprise requires creating repeatable processes and systems rather than depending on individual personnel. He also teaches how to use measurements and innovation and experimentation to stay ahead of the competition.

The book's takeaways and life lessons are:

• Validated learning: Instead of relying on assumptions and gut feelings, entrepreneurs should use experimentation and data to test their consumer and company model assumptions. The text emphasises this.

• The book emphasises the necessity of a continuous feedback loop in which entrepreneurs construct a minimal viable product, measure user reaction, and learn from that feedback to iterate and improve. Build-measure-learn feedback loop.

• Continuous innovation: This book advises business owners to adopt a culture of constant experimentation and learning to stay ahead of the competition and adapt to changing market conditions.

•This book emphasises the importance of recognising when a business idea is not working and being willing to pivot or change course rather than sticking with a failing plan. Unlike the normal practise of persevering with a failing tactic.

• This book emphasises the necessity of understanding customers and actively listening to their comments during product development to design products and services that meet customers' needs and solve their problems.

CHAPTER LXV

"Invent & Wander" by Jeff Bezos

Amazon CEO Jeff Bezos wrote this book. "Invent & Wander" explores Bezos' strategy. Bezos' 20-year yearly shareholder letters are collected in this book. Amazon Shareholder Annual Letters. These letters show how Bezos thinks and approaches growth and innovation.

Bezos emphasises long-term thinking throughout the book as essential to success. He believes that a firm must take chances and make unconventional decisions, even if they don't pay off for years. This requires patience, risk-taking, and a willingness to put long-term goals ahead of short-term profits.

Bezos also emphasises consumer needs first. He believes that focusing on customer needs leads to financial success. He advises firms to listen to customers and improve their services.

Bezos emphasises innovation and experimentation. He thinks firms should try new ideas, even if they fail. He urges firms to try new things and adapt.

The text also stresses adaptability and openness. Bezos stresses the importance of lean organisation and swift pivoting.

Bezos advises companies to relentlessly expand to thrive. He believes organisations should continually seek innovative ways to expand their reach and attract new customers.

The book concludes with the importance of a strong business culture. Bezos believes that a company's culture is its greatest asset and must be nurtured to succeed. He encourages companies to prioritise consumer demands, inventiveness, and experimentation.

In summary, Jeff Bezos is one of the most successful business executives of our time, and "Invent & Wander" reveals his thought process and company concepts. This book emphasises the importance of a strong corporate culture, long-term thinking, customer focus, experimentation and innovation, agility, and sustained growth for business success.

The book's takeaways and life lessons are:

• Long-term thinking: Bezos emphasises long-term thinking while making business decisions. He believes that many firms focus primarily on the short term and that long-term corporate health is essential.

• Amazon's obsession with customers is the key to its success. Bezos believes firms should focus on creating things that benefit customers rather than maximising profits.

• Bezos favours testing and new product development because he believes businesses should continuously be improving their products and services.

Bezos believes that a company's culture is its most valuable asset and that it must encourage innovation, learning, and risk-taking. Bezos considers Amazon's culture a key advantage.

• Diversification: Bezos advises businesses to expand their consumer base and explore new industries to reduce their dependence on one revenue stream.

• Bezos' business philosophy emphasises thrift and cost-cutting. He believes this helps businesses stay focused and avoid distractions.

CHAPTER LXVI

"Business Adventures: The Largest-Selling Business Book of All Time" by John Brooks.

John Brooks‘ "Business Adventures" includes experiences and insights from some of history's most successful business leaders. This book investigates Ford, Xerox, and General Electric's inner workings to highlight their success principles.

This book teaches the value of good leadership. Brooks stresses the need of leaders who can make tough decisions and take calculated risks. He also emphasises having a clear vision and communicating it to employees and stakeholders.

The book also emphasises adaptation. According to Brooks, effective companies can change tactics as necessary rather than sticking to a failing plan.

The book also emphasises teamwork and communication. Brooks says strong companies have a culture of working together and supporting one other, and employees feel free to speak their minds and share their ideas.

In conclusion, Brooks emphasises client focus. He says strong organisations anticipate and address client demands rather than following industry trends.

"Business Adventures" is a fast-paced, informative read. It offers business success tips. Strong leadership, adaptability, teamwork, and a customer-focused strategy are crucial principles.

The book's takeaways and life lessons are:

- Understand and meet your clients' demands.
- Stay ahead by innovating constantly.
- Monitor market trends and adapt.
- Focus on branding and reputation.
- Hire and retain top talent.
- Think big and take calculated risks.
- Manage finances and budgets well.
- Keep learning and improving.
- Have a clear, efficient communication plan.
- Be patient, persistent, and flexible—success takes time and effort.

CHAPTER LXVII

“Digital Minimalism: Choosing a Focused Life in a Noisy World” by Cal Newport

"Digital Minimalism: Choosing a Focused Life in a Noisy World" is a book by computer science professor Cal Newport that argues for the importance of reducing one’s dependence on digital technology and social media in order to live a more focused and fulfilling life. The book is divided into three parts.

In the first part, Newport provides an overview of the problems associated with our increasing use of digital technology, including the negative impact on our attention spans, mental health, and relationships.

In the second part, Newport outlines his philosophy of "digital minimalism," which involves using digital technology in a deliberate and intentional way to support our values and goals, rather than letting it control our lives. He presents a set of practices for implementing digital minimalism, including taking a break from optional technologies, re-evaluating the role of social media in our lives, and prioritizing high-quality leisure activities.

In the final part, Newport explores the benefits of digital minimalism, including increased productivity, better mental health, and a more fulfilling social life. He argues that digital minimalism is not about rejecting technology altogether, but rather about using it in a way that aligns with our values and enhances our lives.

Overall, "Digital Minimalism" provides a persuasive

argument for the importance of reducing our dependence on digital technology and social media in order to live a more focused and fulfilling life. The book offers practical advice and actionable strategies for implementing digital minimalism, making it a useful resource for anyone looking to reduce their digital distractions and live a more intentional life.

The book's takeaways and life lessons are:

- Our increasing use of digital technology and social media can have negative impacts on our attention spans, mental health, and relationships.
- The philosophy of digital minimalism involves using technology in a deliberate and intentional way that aligns with our values and goals.
- Practicing digital minimalism can involve taking a break from optional technologies, re-evaluating the role of social media in our lives, and prioritizing high-quality leisure activities.
- By reducing our dependence on digital distractions, we can increase our productivity, improve our mental health, and have more fulfilling social lives.
- Digital minimalism is not about rejecting technology altogether, but rather about using it in a way that enhances our lives rather than detracts from it.
- The book offers practical advice and actionable strategies for implementing digital minimalism, including conducting a "digital declutter" and prioritizing high-quality leisure activities.

CHAPTER LXVIII

“The Four” is a book by Scott Galloway.

"The Four" by Scott Galloway investigates Amazon, Apple, Facebook, and Google. This book analyses the power of these four digital giants. Scott Galloway is a well-known technology analyst and NYU Stern School of Business marketing lecturer.

The book begins by introducing the "big four," their firms, and their business practises. After that, Galloway explores the many ways these organisations have dominated their areas. He also examines how these companies have maintained market dominance through mergers and alliances.

Galloway also analyses the big four’s data privacy, market concentration, and economic and social impact issues. He also examines the positive and bad effects of these firms‘ domination.

The book’s concept of "network effects" and how particular firms have used them to dominate are key lessons. As more individuals use a product or service, "network effects" increase its value. Galloway shows how these companies used platforms to create network effects and dominate their industries.

Another key idea is data and how these companies have used it to gain a competitive edge. Galloway shows how these companies have used vast amounts of data to better their products and services, target their advertising, and make crucial business decisions.

In addition to these ideas, the book emphasises innovation, adaptability, and long-term thinking in a corporate setting. The author believes that these businesses have succeeded because they are willing to take risks and try new ideas and have the patience to finish their long-term goals.

"The Four" examines the strength and impact of the four biggest technology companies. The author's comprehensive overview of business concepts and tactics that helped the aforementioned organisations climb to prominence covers network effects, data, and branding. The book also emphasises business innovation, adaptation, and long-term thinking. It also raises concerns about these companies' influence and potential repercussions.

The book's takeaways and life lessons are:

• Always put the consumer first: Amazon, Apple, Facebook, and Google know their customers well and use this knowledge to create products and services that meet their needs.

• Create network effects: These companies have built businesses that gain value as more people use them.

• Invest in technology: Each of the four businesses has invested heavily in technology, giving them a market advantage.

• Grow your business: all of these organisations have expanded into new markets and created new revenue streams by looking for opportunities.

• Create a strong brand: Each of these companies has a unique brand that resonates with customers and sets them apart from competitors.

• Be adaptable: These companies can easily adapt to market changes.

- Use data and analytics: All four companies use data and analytics to make decisions to gain a competitive edge.
- Foster innovation: These companies support innovative thinking and original ideas through fostering innovation.
- Be honest: These companies are upfront about their goals, which builds confidence with customers and other stakeholders.

CHAPTER LXIX

“The Personal MBA: Master the Art of Business” by Josh Kaufman.

"The Personal MBA: Master the Art of Business" by Josh Kaufman covers all business essentials. The book’s short and actionable teachings teach modern business fundamentals. The book is a self-guided course.

This book covers business strategy, marketing, sales, negotiation, financial management, and financial administration. Kaufman emphasises the importance of mastering basic business concepts and gives the reader many tips and examples to use these concepts to their own firms or jobs.

The book breaks down value creation as a core premise. Kaufman emphasises the importance of customer value and explains how organisations may do this by understanding their target market’s needs and producing products and services to meet them.

Leverage is another key concept in the book. Kaufman uses examples to show how organisations can get a competitive edge by exploiting their resources and competencies. He also provides practical advise on finding and maximising market impact opportunities.

This book also addresses financial management, including budgeting, forecasting, and performance evaluation. Kaufman emphasises understanding and using financial facts to make informed business decisions.

Kaufman invites readers to "take action" and apply the book’s principles to their careers throughout the book. He provides exercises and references to help readers apply the book's ideas.

This book covers understanding the value proposition, providing value for customers, leveraging resources and capabilities, financial management, budgeting, forecasting, assessing performance, and taking action to execute the acquired concepts. Leveraging resources and abilities is another important lesson.

The book's takeaways and life lessons are:

• Understand business fundamentals including value development, client acquisition, and financial management.
• Learn to analyse and solve business problems using frameworks and models.
• Prioritize practical skills over theoretical knowledge.
•Find new information and resources to improve your business skills and stay ahead of the competition.
• Recognize and commit to trial and error in building a successful firm.
• Always be learning and open to new ideas.
• Understand how marketing drives business performance and how to communicate value to customers.
• Understand the consumer, their needs, and the best way to communicate and provide value.
• Learn how to create and follow a budget, analyse financial data, and make decisions based on empirical evidence.
• Recognize the importance of leadership and management in building a successful firm and learn how to lead and manage others.

CHAPTER LXX

"Coffee Can Investing: The Low Risk Route to Stupendous Wealth" by Saurabh Mukherjea.

"Coffee Can Investing: The Low Risk Route to Stupendous Wealth" author Saurabh Mukherjea studies value investing in the Indian stock market. Saurabh Mukherjea is a stock market analyst and investment counsellor with over twenty years of experience.

The book shows how value investing—buying inexpensive stocks with excellent fundamentals and keeping them for the long term—can yield high returns with low risk. Value investing involves long-term holding of cheap stocks with excellent fundamentals. The author describes a portfolio of securities as a "coffee can" that investors should preserve regardless of market volatility until the stocks reach their intrinsic value.

This book covers value investing in chapters. The book introduces value investing and its differences from other investment methods. The author then discusses the importance of understanding a company's balance sheet, income statement, and cash flow statement. He also emphasises researching a company's management, competitive position, and growth possibilities.

This book also discusses "economic moats," a company's long-term competitive advantages that ensure profitability and market domination. The author shows that economic moats help enterprises survive market downturns and retain ROI.

The author also explains the Indian stock market, which may be useful to investors contemplating India. He also provides a list of "coffee can" equities, which he believes will yield high returns over time.

"Coffee May Investing" is a comprehensive guide on value investing in the Indian stock market. This book provides a plethora of information and ideas for long-term, low-risk investors.

The book's takeaways and life lessons are:

• Find undervalued high-quality businesses

• The author emphasises finding businesses with strong fundamentals, a competitive edge, and a sustainable business plan. These companies are more likely to survive market downturns and generate long-term profits.

Long-term investing

• The author believes long-term investing in firms yields the best profits. Long-term company investments multiply returns. This method reduces risk while offering compounding opportunities.

• Diversify: The author suggests diversifying across markets and industries to mitigate risk and volatility. This prevents a portfolio company or industry from being overweighted.

• Patience and self-control: This requires repressing emotional responses to market changes and sticking to a long-term investing strategy, no matter how illogical market conditions seem.

• Educate yourself on the market and your investments. This article advises investors to invest in themselves by learning about the market and their companies. This can help investors make better decisions and anticipate market movements.

CHAPTER LXXI

“One Up On Wall Street: How To Use What You Already Know To Make Money In The Market” by Peter Lynch and John Rothchild.

"One Up On Wall Street" is a guide to Peter Lynch’s investment philosophy and tactics, and it explains how he managed the Fidelity Magellan Fund for 13 years with an average annual return of 29%.

Each section covers a different aspect of Lynch’s investment philosophy. This chapter begins with Lynch’s investment technique, which emphasises knowing the company whose stocks you’re considering buying. Lynch believes the key to investing success is finding great companies with trustworthy management teams and buying their equities at reasonable prices.

Lynch’s investment method—how he seeks new assets, conducts research, and evaluates firms—is examined in the book’s second part. Lynch advises studying a company’s finances, products, and management before investing. He also emphasises having a long-term investment plan and avoiding stock market volatility.

The book’s conclusion illustrates Lynch’s investment theory. These examples are case studies of various firms he invested in successfully. These case studies explain Lynch’s investment strategy and how he found high-growth companies. Lynch identified high-growth firms, making him a profitable investor.

"One Up On Wall Street" is a must-read for everyone

interested in Lynch's financial strategies. This book analyses Lynch's investment strategy and teaches how to spot and capitalise on great company prospects.

The book's takeaways and life lessons are:

• Invest in what you know: Lynch emphasises investing in companies and industries one is familiar with rather than picking stocks based on insider information or expert opinion. Use your expertise and research to find companies with good fundamentals and long-term success.

• Lynch discusses "moats," or a company's capacity to maintain a competitive advantage over time. Investors should search for deep and wide moats. He believes that companies with a competitive advantage, such as a well-known brand, patents, or economies of scale, will succeed over time.

• Pay attention to management: Lynch stresses that a company's management team and how they run the organisation can predict its future success.

• Avoid hot or overhyped stocks: Lynch advises avoiding investing in media- or expert-hyped stocks since they may be overvalued and lose value. He also stresses the importance of patience and long-term stock holding rather than frequent stock trading.

• Expect uncertainty: Lynch acknowledges that the stock market is unpredictable and that stock values can fluctuate quickly. Thus, investors should expect volatility. He cautions readers to expect volatility and not make hasty judgements based on short-term market movements.

CHAPTER LXXII

"Common Stocks and Uncommon Profits" by Philip A. Fisher

"Common Stocks and Uncommon Profits" is by Philip A. Fisher, a successful investor of the 20th century. Fisher is the book's title character. The 1958 book has become an investing classic.

This book describes Fisher's investment strategy. He recommends investing in companies with strong foundations, a competitive edge, and qualified management. He emphasises thorough investigation and appropriate diligence. He also stresses the need of understanding a company's sector and growth prospects.

Fisher encourages "scuttlebutt," or chatting to people in a business to learn about it. He believes investors may learn about a company via its suppliers, consumers, and competitors. He's optimistic.

Fisher advises financial decision-making with patience and self-control. Instead than trying to time the market, he advises investors to choose good companies and stay onto them. Contrary to market timing. He also advises against overdiversification and suggests focusing on a few reputable companies.

"Common Stocks and Uncommon Profits" provides a detailed and practical investment plan. Before investing, do extensive study, due diligence, and understand the industry and firm. It also stresses patience, discipline, and long-term thinking while investing in stocks.

The book's takeaways and life lessons are:

- Fisher recommends researching a company's management, products, and industry before investing. This research should inform your decision. He advises readers to consider a company's financial statistics, competitive position, development potential, and managerial quality.
- Fisher emphasises long-term stock investing. He believes investors should focus on a company's long-term prospects rather than trying to time the market.
- Diversification: Fisher advises investors to diversify their portfolios by investing in companies in diverse markets. He believes diversity reduces risk and protects an investor's portfolio from one stock's success.
- Patience: Fisher recommends long-term investors to be patient. According to him, patient and disciplined stock market investors are more likely to succeed. He contrasts this with hasty, narrow-minded investors.
- Fisher advises stock investors to maintain a safety margin. He advises investors to only invest in companies whose shares are trading at a significant discount to their fundamental value to avoid stock price losses.

CHAPTER LXXIII

“The Intelligent Investor” by Benjamin Graham

Finance and investing scholars consider Benjamin Graham’s "The Intelligent Investor" a classic. Since 1949, the book has been rewritten several times. The book teaches value investing basics and long-term investing skills.

The book’s key premise is "margin of safety," the difference between a company’s intrinsic value and its market price. The book recommends readers to invest in stocks with a high profit margin to reduce the risk of financial loss.

The book also discusses "Mr. Market," a fictional figure who represents the stock market and its fluctuations. The book advocates focusing on a firm’s long-term value rather than market volatility.

The book also examines portfolio diversification and investment planning elements. It also emphasises the importance of patience, discipline, and avoiding emotional decisions when investing.

One of the book’s most essential lessons is that stock investing requires extensive research and analysis. The book’s author advises readers to analyse the company’s management, financial statements, industry trends, and competitors before choosing.

"The Intelligent Investor" advises investors to avoid market volatility and have a long-term view. It also stresses the importance of diversifying investing portfolios and not making quick judgements.

"The Intelligent Investor" is for anyone who wants to learn more about the stock market and investing. For value investors, this book is a must-read.

The book's takeaways and life lessons are:

• Value investing: Graham emphasises finding undervalued stocks rather than chasing after overvalued ones. This is unlike investing in stocks that have already appreciated.
• Graham recommends diversification to reduce risk. He advises diversifying into stocks, bonds, and other assets.
• Patience and self-control: Graham emphasises patience and self-control when investing to avoid market speculation.
• Margin of Safety: Graham coined the term, which is the difference between a stock's market price and its intrinsic value. It mitigates inherent value estimation errors. Graham emphasises the need of analysing a company's financial statements to assess its health and growth potential.
• Graham advises investors to avoid speculating and focus on long-term investments in stable companies.
• Graham advises investors not to buy or sell a firm based on market rumours or news. Avoiding impulsive decisions helps avoid emotional ones. He suggests investors base their decisions on thorough research and analysis.
• Long-Term Focus Graham advises investors to focus on a company's long-term prospects rather than market fluctuations.
• Graham states that an investment must have a margin of safety whereas a speculation must be backed by hope. Financial decisions should consider this distinction.

CHAPTER LXXIV

“The Little Book of Common Sense Investing: The Only Way to Guarantee Your Fair Share of Stock Market Returns” by John C. Bogle

Vanguard Group founder and index fund creator John C. Bogle wrote "The Little Book of Common Sense Investing." Bogle wrote this book. This book teaches private investors how to earn from stock market investing. The book advocates investing in a low-cost, diversified index fund that tracks the market rather than trying to beat it.

This book begins with a history of investment practises and the stock market. Bogle then explains index funds, which track a market index like the S&P 500. Bogle’s index fund explanation is below. He believes index funds are better for individual investors than actively managed funds since they have reduced expenses and risk.

Bogle emphasises investing diversity. He advises diversifying across asset classes and businesses to reduce risk. He also advises on choosing the finest index fund and calculating the appropriate asset distribution for an investment portfolio.

This book’s most essential lesson is to constantly consider long-term goals when buying stock. Bogle advises investors to invest for the long term and use compounding to their advantage.

The book also discusses minimising expenses. Bogle recommends low-expense index funds since high fees and expenses can reduce returns.

"The Little Book of Common Sense Investing" emphasises investing in low-cost, diversified index funds, taking a long-term view, and minimising costs. The book emphasises cost-cutting. This book teaches readers how to choose an index fund and calculate their portfolio's asset allocation.

The book's takeaways and life lessons are:

• A low-cost diversified index fund is the best long-term investment strategy.

• The stock market's efficiency makes it hard for individual investors to consistently beat it with active stock selection or market timing.

• Emotions and biases may lead investors to bad financial decisions. Instead of reacting to short-term market swings, have a long-term investing plan and stick to it. Long-term investment plans can prevent costly mistakes.

• Compounding can make low-cost index funds profitable over time.

• Profitable investing involves minimising expenses and taxes and letting compounding do the rest.

• Avoid high-performing investments and market timing and set reasonable investment returns.

• When it comes to risk management in an investing portfolio, diversification is absolutely necessary.

• The long-term effectiveness of an investment strategy relies heavily on both patience and discipline.

• Investing in a diverse portfolio of low-cost index funds and holding onto them for the long run is the most effective strategy to attain success in one's financial investments over the long term.

• Investing successfully requires a patient approach over the long run and a focus on minimising costs as much as possible.

CHAPTER LXXV

“The Most Important Thing: Uncommon Sense for the Thoughtful Investor” by Howard Marks

"The Most Important Thing: Uncommon Sense for the Thoughtful Investor" by Howard Marks is a thorough stock market and investing handbook. The first half covers the stock market and how it operates, while the second gives practical advice on how to invest. Both parts cover the stock market.

This book emphasises understanding and managing risk. Investors must maximise returns and minimise losses, according to Marks. He emphasises the importance of having a clear investing plan and sticking to it despite market volatility.

Another of Marks‘ concepts is long-term thinking. He believes short-term investors are more likely to act rashly and be mislead by market noise. He advises a deliberate approach that prioritises a company’s long-term growth.

Marks emphasises the importance of thinking for oneself and not following the herd. He believes that investors who can think critically and make their conclusions on their own research and analysis are more likely to succeed.

The book also offers advice on analysing firms and investing. Marks’ approach can assess a company’s management and financial statements. He also advises against common financial mistakes like overpaying for a stock or following the latest trend.

"The Most Important Thing" is a comprehensive

investment reference. It contains useful information and advice. It emphasises risk management, long-term thinking, independence, and avoiding investing mistakes.

The book's takeaways and life lessons are:

• "Second-level thinking"—going beyond the obvious and considering the opposite view—to make smarter investing judgements.
• Understanding cycles and that markets and economies are always changing.
• Rather than trying to timing the market or follow hot stocks, it's crucial to have a disciplined and consistent investment approach. Risk and return are strongly related, and increasing one's exposure to risk may result in better returns but requires a wider margin of safety to defend against loss. This is where the value lies.
• The importance of regulating one's emotions and avoiding market euphoria or panic.
Diversification helps spread risk across investment categories and company sectors.
• The importance of long-term thinking and constancy amid market volatility.
• Understand a company's basic competencies and values before buying its stock.
• The need for patience and discipline to succeed in long-term investing. • The need for continual education and market updates.

CHAPTER LXXVI

“Never Split the Difference: Negotiating As If Your Life Depended On It” by Chris Voss

"Never Split the Difference: Negotiating As If Your Life Depended On It" by FBI hostage negotiator Chris Voss. The author’s experience in high-stakes negotiations gives readers a new perspective on how to negotiate successfully in any situation.

The book is divided into three sections: the first covers negotiation fundamentals and the author’s framework for understanding how to negotiate successfully; the second covers negotiation psychology and how to read people, build rapport, and establish trust; and the third covers advanced negotiation tactics and provides real-life examples of how these tactics have been successfully applied in a variety of situations.

"Mirroring" is another important topic the author discusses. To build rapport and make the other person feel understood, this technique involves repeating a few of their recent statements.

Voss also discusses "labelling," which involves acknowledging and validating another person’s emotions.

Voss also offers ways to handle hostile negotiation partners, emotional outbursts, and negotiation deadlocks.

The book provides a framework for understanding negotiation psychology and practical skills that can be used in many situations. The book is also useful. Active listening, mirroring, labelling, understanding the other party’s

BATNA, and managing difficult situations are guiding principles.

The book's takeaways and life lessons are:

• Negotiation requires empathy. Understanding the other person's perspective and feelings will help you predict their actions and tailor your approach to their needs.
• Active listening is crucial to bargaining. Listening attentively can help you learn and connect with others.
• Labelling can reduce tension and increase comprehension. Acknowledging and validating the other side's feelings can help you find a compromise.
• Mirroring builds trust and rapport. Repeating the other person's last few words shows you're listening and builds rapport.
• Tactical empathy is the ability to recognise and influence the other party's feelings without compromising one's own interests.
• The "Accusation Audit" can identify and defuse critiques or charges against a person or organisation. Acknowledge and address the other party's worries to prevent them from worsening and solve the problem.
• "No" has power in negotiations. Strategically stating "no" sets boundaries and expresses priorities.
• "Calibrated Questions" is a method for learning and understanding. Asking open-ended questions will help you learn more and understand the other party.
• The "Amplifying" approach can be used to understand and influence the other party. Restating and embellishing their statement can help you understand and influence it.

CHAPTER LXXVII

"Surrounded by Idiots: The Four Types of Human Behavior " by Thomas Erikson

"Surrounded by Idiots: The Four Types of Human Behavior" was written by Swedish communication expert and consultant Thomas Erikson. Erikson wrote this book using his experience and extensive research in communication and behaviour. This book helps readers understand and navigate their personal and professional behaviour patterns.

Red, blue, green, and yellow behaviour will be covered. The book describes how to interact with each of the colours' behaviours and mentalities.

Red personalities have strong emotions, impulsivity, and a quick response. Red people are impulsive, direct, and energetic. Erikson advises being direct and forceful with red personalities to match their energy and intensity.

Blue people are rational and analytical. Blue people are rational and objective. In addition to this, people have the impression that they are level-headed, unruffled, and not easily moved by their feelings. To gain the trust and respect of blue personality types, Erikson advises being analytical and data-driven.

Greens are cooperative and empathic. Green people are empathetic, supportive, and good listeners. They are also known for being empathetic and accommodating. Erikson believes that empathising and understanding green worldview people is essential to building trust and connection.

Yellow conduct types think creatively. Yellows are creative, versatile, and open-minded. Yellow behaviour is innovative. They also appear independent. Erikson advises being open-minded and supportive of yellow people to encourage creativity and innovation. Yellow individuals require this.

Erikson uses many scenarios and examples to demonstrate different behavioural patterns and the best ways to interact with them. He also stresses the need of self-awareness and how others may perceive one's actions.

The book's takeaways and life lessons are:

• Empathy: The tale encourages empathy when interacting with others. By understanding others' perspectives and striving to put oneself in their shoes, people can better understand and improve their own behaviour.

• Adaptability: The author stresses the importance of adaptability and flexibility in working with diverse groups.

• The book emphasises the importance of clear and effective communication in building and maintaining healthy relationships. Knowing others' behaviour helps people converse effectively.

• Self-awareness: The author advises readers to consider how their actions affect others. Self-awareness entails understanding how your actions affect others. If they understand their behaviour and how others see it, people can improve their relationships.

• Understanding others' behaviour is stressed throughout the book to help solve problems and make collaborative decisions.

CHAPTER LXXVIII

“How to Talk to Anyone: 92 Little Tricks for Big Success in Relationships” by Leil Lowndes.

Leil Lowndes' book "How to Talk to Anyone: 92 Little Tricks for Big Success in Relationships" covers all aspects of communication. Chapters cover topics like how to handle difficult conversations, how to build relationships, and how to make a good first impression.

The book argues that understanding and connecting with others is more important than giving a polished presentation. The author emphasises nonverbal signs and body language in communication and offers tips for improving them.

The book also discusses negotiating, talking to powerful people, and handling criticism. The book focuses on talking to influential people. It also covers dispute resolution and dealing with difficult people.

The book taught me that successful communication isn’t just about words, but about understanding and connecting with others. It also emphasises how nonverbal clues and body language may build connection and trust.

Effective communication requires practise and a willingness to be vulnerable. The author encourages readers to use the book’s methods, accept comments, and reflect.

"How to Talk to Anyone" is a practical guide that helps readers improve their communication skills and build stronger relationships with those around them.

The book's takeaways and life lessons are:

• Show that you care. Question and listen to the other person to connect.
• Ask open-ended questions to get personal information.
• Mirroring the other person's body language and repeating key sentences shows you're listening.
• Storytelling may improve your argument and keep the conversation interesting.
• Use body language to show openness and confidence.
• Humor others to bond.
• Use their name and chat to put them at ease.
•Use the "Magic of Three" to shape and fluidize your speech.
• Use your tone of voice when speaking.
• Actively listen and focus on understanding the other person.

CHAPTER LXXIX

“The Quick and Easy Way to Effective Speaking” by Dale Carnegie.

Carnegie’s "The Quick and Easy Way to Effective Speaking" teaches public speaking and communication. This book gives readers actionable tips to become more confident and persuasive public speakers.

The text emphasises knowing one’s target demographic. Carnegie stresses the significance of tailoring one’s message to the audience to have better impact. He also stresses the need of speaking honestly rather than pretending to be someone else.

Another book principle is preparation. Carnegie advises researching and practising your speech to prepare. "How to Win Friends and Influence People" contains Carnegie’s advice. He emphasises the importance of being aware of one’s body language and nonverbal clues and using them strategically to attain goals.

The book also discusses ways to overcome stage fear, such as deep breathing and visualising success. Carnegie also suggests using narrative and stories to make your speech more engaging and memorable.

The book offers a number of methods for improving public speaking skills. It emphasises knowing one’s audience, being sincere, and thoroughly preparing for a speech. It also offers speech preparation and nerve-calming techniques.

The book’s takeaways and life lessons are:

• Speak from the heart: Carnegie emphasises honesty and authenticity when giving a speech.

• Carnegie advises public speakers to speak conversationally and use their own language rather than trying to remember their speeches. He advises researching your audience and using examples and stories that resonate with them.

• Use simple language: Carnegie advises avoiding jargon, technical terms, and huge words. He believes simple language can help you connect with your audience and persuade them.

• Carnegie says storytelling may connect with an audience and make a speech memorable. He suggests using tales, parables, and examples to make your points clearer.

• Carnegie emphasises practise for public speaking. Public speakers should practise in front of a mirror or with a friend to gain feedback and improve their performance.

• Be Confident: Carnegie teaches his students to be confident and not worry about public speaking faults. He believes confidence is needed to deliver a speech and engage the audience.

• Be Cheerful: Carnegie advises speakers to be positive and enthusiastic to create a positive mood and make the audience more receptive. Carnegie advises speaking positively.

• Carnegie advises utilising comedy to lighten the mood and make the audience more receptive. He advises public speakers to entertain audiences with jokes, puns, and stories.

• Carnegie advises presenters to be themselves rather than imitate others. He believes everyone has a unique speaking style and should embrace it.

CHAPTER LXXX

"Power Questions: Build Relationships, Win New Business, and Influence Others" by Andrew Sobel and Jerold Panas.

Jerold Panas and Andrew Sobel wrote "Power Questions: Build Relationships, Win New Business, and Influence Others." This book helps businesses and individuals improve communication and relationships. Buy it here. The writers believe that asking insightful questions is crucial to success in any endeavour, whether personal or professional. The book has three parts: developing relationships, acquiring new clients, and influencing others.

The first chapter emphasises the importance of developing relationships through thought-provoking questions. Asking the right questions can help people understand others, gain confidence, and form strong bonds, according to the authors.

The second part of the book discusses acquiring new customers by asking questions to understand their needs and motivations.

In the book's third section, compelling questions influence others. Asking the right questions can give people insight into others' thoughts and motivations, which they can use to influence them. The authors present methods for formulating questions to help individuals and corporations achieve their goals and gain influence.

They also provide a list of insightful questions that

individuals and businesses can use in various contexts. The book's clear, straightforward writing makes it easy for readers to understand and apply its strategies.

This book emphasises the need of building relationships, understanding potential consumers' needs and motives, and using questions to influence others. It also stresses the importance of understanding the other person's perspective and tailoring inquiries to that perspective to get the desired results.

The book's takeaways and life lessons are:

• Strong relationships are vital for business and life success. Thought-provoking questions can build trust, gather knowledge, and influence others.
• The right question is crucial. Each inquiry has a different goal.
• Long-term partnerships require active listening and follow-up.
• Showing genuine interest in others and trying to understand their perspectives builds strong bonds.
• Open-ended questions encourage debate, whereas closed-ended questions provide specific facts.
• Ask "What Else?" to find further possibilities and needs.
• Asking "How" can reveal someone's mental process or behaviours.
• Use "What If" to encourage creative thinking and possibility exploration.
• Asking "Who" may reveal key players and potential friends.

CHAPTER LXXXI

“How to Win Friends and Influence People” by Dale Carnegie

Dale Carnegie’s "How to Win Friends and Influence People" is a timeless personal development book. Since 1936, the book has sold over 30 million copies worldwide. Carnegie focuses on effective communication and human psychology to help readers build and maintain relationships.

Carnegie divides this book into four sections: "Fundamentals of Handling People," "Six Ways to Make People Like You," "How to Win People to Your Way of Thinking," and "Be a Leader: How to Change People Without Giving Offense or Arousing Resentment." These parts cover several aspects of Carnegie’s main theme, "How to Win People to Your Way of Thinking."

Carnegie emphasises human behaviour psychology in the book’s introduction. He also shows how to connect with people by genuinely caring about their needs and wants. He recommends active listening and not criticising, complaining, or judging.

Carnegie’s second portion offers six ways to win people over. These include being truly interested in others, smiling, remembering names, listening well, talking about others‘ interests, and making others feel valued.

This article’s third section explains how to influence others. Carnegie stresses the importance of knowing the other person, using logic and reason to argue, and avoiding disputes. He also suggests using stories and anecdotes to explain your points.

In the book's second half, Carnegie shows how to lead by changing people's attitudes and behaviour without offending or resenting them. He tells readers to use praise and encouragement instead of criticism to build others up. "How to Win Friends and Influence People" covers communication and psychology basics. The book is a valuable resource for anybody seeking to improve their relationships since it offers direct and easy guidance.

The book's takeaways and life lessons are:

• Taking a genuine interest in others and learning to see things from their perspective
• listening attentively and showing empathy
• calling someone by their name while talking to them
• complimenting someone in a straightforward and genuine way
• acknowledging people's mistakes in a non-threatening way Avoid confrontations and respect others' beliefs. Acknowledge people's faults in a non-threatening way
• Encourage and congratulate others
• Limit harsh and critical comments Question instead of ordering.
• Making someone feel valued and respected
• Building confidence and dependability
• encouraging optimism and excitement

CHAPTER LXXXII

"How to Develop Self-Confidence and Influence People by Public Speaking" by Dale Carnegie.

Carnegie starts by discussing how self-confidence is essential for success in any field. He then describes his many public speaking anxiety-reduction methods. He emphasises preparation, audience focus, and simple language.

Carnegie advises focusing on the audience and knowing their needs. He advises speakers to examine what their audience wants to learn and structure their remarks accordingly. He emphasises being simple and succinct and avoiding jargon and technical terms that may confuse the audience.

Carnegie also stressed preparation. He advises public speakers to practise, learn key concepts, and deliver. He also advocates using slides and props to improve the message and engage the audience.

Carnegie uses real-world examples and in-depth case studies throughout the book. He also covers how to handle audience inquiries and pre-speech anxiety.

"How to Develop Self-Confidence and Influence People by Public Speaking" is a must-read for public speakers. This comprehensive resource contains advice and methods. This article is essential for anyone wanting to improve their public speaking skills.

The book's takeaways and life lessons are:

• Preparing for and practising public speaking to boost self-confidence.

• Using conversational language to connect with the audience and personalise the speech.

• Using personal tales to demonstrate themes and engage the audience.

• Making a good first impression and connecting with the audience.

• Enhancing speech delivery via gestures, voice modulation, and facial emotions.

• The importance of effectively gauging audience needs and modifying presentations accordingly.

•Humor to lighten the mood and improve the speech.

• The importance of ending the speech with a strong call to action or memorable conclusion.

• Focusing on the listener and the issue to overcome uncertainty and nervousness.

•To improve as a public speaker, one must practise often.

CHAPTER LXXXIII

“The Communication Book: 44 Ideas for Better Conversations Every Day” by Mikael Krogerus and Roman Tschäppeler.

"The Communication Book: 44 Ideas for Better Conversations Every Day" by Mikael Krogerus and Roman Tschappeler gives tips for improving daily communication. This book has 44 chapters on different communication topics. These chapters explain how to start discussions, make small talk, dispute politely, and give feedback.

The authors use a variety of studies and examples throughout the book. They shed light on communication psychology and nonverbal cues. They emphasise attentive listening and open-ended questions.

The book’s main point is that fruitful talks require putting oneself in the other person’s shoes. The writers stress the need of being sensitive to others' feelings, interests, and needs and adapting one’s communication style accordingly. Another fundamental tenet is "meta-communication," or the message beneath the one being expressed. Effective communication includes language, tone, and surroundings, according to the writers. They encourage readers to focus on their message and nonverbal cues.

The book also offers helpful communication tips and exercises. The authors advise keeping a conversation notebook to record and reflect on encounters and how to prepare for difficult conversations and presentations.

The "Communication Book" is a comprehensive guide to

enhancing communication skills in all areas of life. It provides practical advice, ideas, and examples to help readers understand communication and improve their skills.

The book's takeaways and life lessons are:

- The value of active listening and asking open-ended questions
- The importance of open, direct, and plain communication
- The relevance of narrative in communication
- Using nonverbal communication strategies like body language and facial expressions to improve verbal communication
- The impact of power dynamics on communication and the importance of recognising and resolving them
- The importance of being flexible in one's communication style and being able to adapt to the circumstance and person one is conversing with
- The importance and necessity of being able to control and effectively transmit one's sentiments in communication
- The usefulness of humour in communication and the ability to use it to establish connections and defuse unpleasant situations

CHAPTER LXXXIV

"Talk Like TED: The 9 Public-Speaking Secrets of the World's Top Minds" by Carmine Gallo.

"Talk Like TED: The 9 Public-Speaking Secrets of the World's Top Minds" by Carmine Gallo is a book about public speaking inspired by some of the world's most famous TED presenters. The book reveals how these speakers captivated audiences and gave effective, persuasive, and memorable presentations.

Public speaking narrative is the book's first topic. It emphasises that relatable, honest storytelling is the key to connecting with your audience. It then discusses the importance of creating a clear and appealing message and tailoring your language and delivery style to your audience. This book also explains how to use body language and other nonverbal communication to reinforce your message and build audience trust. It also emphasises preparation, inquiry, and using facts, numbers, and research to strengthen your case.

The book teaches that honesty and vulnerability are crucial to public speaking. The book advises public speakers to be honest and open about their personal struggles to build trust and a deeper connection with their audience.

The book also emphasises the importance of using jokes, anecdotes, and analogies in public speaking to engage audiences and reinforce crucial points. It also emphasises the importance of using multimedia and visual aids to reinforce and persuade.

"Talk Like TED: The 9 Public-Speaking Secrets of the World's Top Minds" by Carmine Gallo is a comprehensive handbook to public speaking. World-renowned TED presenters inspire the author. This part covers storytelling, clear and persuasive messaging, body language and nonverbal communication, research and preparation, honesty and vulnerability, humour, stories, examples, multimedia, and visual aids.

The book's takeaways and life lessons are:

- The importance of carefully composing a coherent and persuasive message that resonates with the target audience
- The power of storytelling in public speaking, particularly in terms of how it can captivate and win over the audience
- The use of nonverbal communication to strengthen the message and gain the audience's trust
- The need of regular rehearsals and preparation for a professional and confident presentation
- Humor and vulnerability help connect with audiences and clarify messages.
- Being aware of one's target demographic to appropriately adapt one's message
- Applying evidence in the form of statistics, data, and research to back up and lend credibility to the message
- Using different types of media and other visual aids to strengthen the message and make it easier to recall
- Maintaining one's integrity and authenticity at all times.

CHAPTER LXXXV

“Crucial Conversations: Tools for Talking When Stakes Are High, Second Edition” by Kerry Patterson, Joseph Grenny, Ron McMillan, and Al Switzler.

"Crucial Interactions: Tools for Talking When Stakes Are High, Second Edition" helps readers navigate high-stakes conversations. Kerry Patterson, Joseph Grenny, Ron McMillan, and Al Switzler’s book argues that essential discussions are high-stakes, emotionally intense, and can change a person’s life. Kerry Patterson, Joseph Grenny, and Al Switzler wrote the book. The book will teach the reader how to communicate in these situations.

This book’s main point is that people often avoid essential conversations out of fear of rejection, fighting, or losing respect. The authors argue that postponing critical talks usually leads to inferior long-term outcomes, making this anxiety unfounded and wasteful. They say this dread is unnecessary.

The book’s author states that open, honest communication and listening to the other person’s perspective are the keys to navigating uncomfortable conversations.

The book also stresses the importance of being positive and respectful in difficult conversations. This enhances dialogue and maintains good connections, according to the authors.

"Crucial Conversations: Tools for Talking When Stakes Are

High, Second Edition" teaches readers how to communicate in high-stakes situations. The book emphasises the importance of being able to convey one's thoughts and feelings in a simple and true manner, as well as listening to and understanding another person's position while remaining positive and respectful.

The book's takeaways and life lessons are:

• The book emphasises the importance of "crucial talks" to build relationships, solve problems, and achieve goals.
• "Crucial discussions" are high-stakes, emotional, and potentially life-changing conversations. Their book establishes this.
• The book covers how to prepare, initiate, regulate emotions, and establish common ground in key conversations.
• The authors also discuss ways to keep a discourse going even when you disagree.
• The book also emphasises the importance of communicating clearly and compassionately while respecting others.
• The book also discusses forgiving and apologising. This book also discusses the significance of recognising and managing emotions and stress during communication.
• The book emphasises the importance of open and honest communication to build trust and respect in relationships.

CHAPTER LXXXVI

"The Art of Living" by Epictetus

Epictetus, a Stoic philosopher, wrote "The Art of Living," a guide to moral and contented living. The book's main message is that the only way to find true pleasure and freedom is to first recognise and accept one's own limitations and then focus on one's own actions and attitudes rather than external circumstances. Epictetus emphasises self-discipline, rational thought, and morality for a good life. He also emphasises embracing nature and living in harmony with it. He recommends self-discipline, introspection, and inner tranquilly. He also emphasises the need of conducting one's life according to reason and virtue and in harmony with others.

The book's main assumption is that people can regulate their ideas, feelings, and happiness. Epictetus believes that how we react to events, not the events themselves, determines our happiness. He recommends awareness and living in the now rather than stressing about the past or future. He also stresses the importance of letting go of worldly possessions and external circumstances, which we cannot control.

Virtue and morality are also fundamental to the text. Epictetus advises readers to cultivate virtue and live ethically. He believes that only a moral life and a rational path can bring true happiness. He also emphasises kindness, compassion, and respect.

Epictetus, an ancient Stoic philosopher, wrote "The Art of Living," a collection of his teachings on how to live a good life. The book's fundamental idea is that one may only feel true joy and liberation after realising and accepting life's restrictions, focusing on their own actions and attitudes, and living according to reason and virtue. This philosophy emphasises virtue, morality, living in the present, and letting go of ties to material possessions and external events.

The book's takeaways and life lessons are:

- Epictetus popularised the Stoic idea of accepting one's fate and making the best of it.
- Epictetus believed that focusing on one's own deeds and attitudes rather than external occurrences was the path to happiness.
- Epictetus emphasises self-discipline and self-control for inner calm.
- To overcome life's inevitable problems, he emphasises inner fortitude and resiliency.
- Epictetus emphasises following one's reason and virtue and avoiding behaviours that go against one's values.
- He advises practising mindfulness and living in the now rather than worrying about the past or future.
- Epictetus advises cultivating thanks and contentment rather than continuously seeking improvement.
- He emphasises the importance of living a simple, modest life without the distractions and excesses of owning a lot of material possessions.
- Epictetus encourages others to pursue wisdom and self-improvement as the peak of accomplishment.

CHAPTER LXXXVII

"The Courage to Be Disliked" by Ichiro Kishimi and Fumitake Koga

Ichiro Kishimi and Fumitake Koga's self-help book "The Courage to Be Disliked" examines Epictetus's concepts and how they might be applied to modern living. A young man and a philosopher talk about the book. The philosopher teaches the youth Epictetus' Stoic philosophy.

The book emphasises the importance of taking responsibility for one's own thoughts and feelings rather than allowing others influence them. It also stresses the need of being honest with oneself and living by one's own values rather than trying to please others or conform to society.

This book discusses "philosophical detachment," the ability to emotionally and intellectually isolate oneself from other people's feelings and perspectives and not let them influence one's own judgements and actions. The book also advises readers to focus on the parts of their lives they can control and not waste mental energy worrying about things they can't change.

Another key notion is "the inner citadel," which means having a strong sense of self that is unaffected by outside circumstances. This idea emphasises having a strong self-image. This inner citadel is built on inner strength, emotional intelligence, and autonomy. Another theme in the book is that the reader should take responsibility for their own pleasure and well-being rather than relying on others.

"The Courage to Be Disliked" encourages readers to take responsibility for their thoughts and emotions, be loyal to themselves, and live by their own beliefs rather than striving to please others or adapt to society. This book inspires readers to own their thoughts and feelings. This book emphasises the importance of self-awareness, honesty, and the "inner citadel" as a location to develop inner fortitude, emotional intelligence, and independent thought.

The book's takeaways and life lessons are:

- The book interprets Aristotelianism, which holds that humans are innately social and that happiness depends on our relationships.
- The authors argue that we can only evolve as individuals by accepting who we are and accepting that acceptance in its whole. Self-acceptance underpins the text.
- The book emphasises "courage" in facing our fears and overcoming them and taking responsibility for our thoughts, feelings, and actions.
- Cognitive dissonance, which occurs when our beliefs and actions conflict, is explained. Discomfort or tension comes when our beliefs and actions collide.
- To get a deeper understanding of oneself and the world, the book encourages readers to challenge their preconceptions and ideas.
- The writers recommend a "philosophical attitude" towards life, which involves taking a step back and reflecting on our experiences and emotions to better comprehend the world and our place in it. Thus, the authors encourage a "philosophical perspective" towards life.

- The book also stresses the importance of being present and aware of one's actions and thoughts.
- It also encourages readers to adjust their lives to better their relationships and well-being.

CHAPTER LXXXVIII

"Beyond Good and Evil" by Friedrich Nietzsche

Nietzsche's "Beyond Good and Evil" explores morality, knowledge, and power. This book's chapters cover many topics. In the first section of his book, Nietzsche argues that traditional morality—based on good and evil—is a product of power. He claims that humans invented good and evil and that there is no objective morality. Nietzsche claims that the traditional morality of Christianity and other religions is oppression and that the only way to achieve true freedom is to overthrow it. Nietzsche feels this is the only road to full freedom.

Nietzsche critiques truth in the second section of his article, arguing that knowing is based on power. He believes truth is a human invention used to justify power. Humans must create truth, according to Nietzsche. He thinks science and philosophy produce truth rather than discover it.

Nietzsche's third essay criticises reason as a product of power. He claims that reason produces truth rather than uncovering it. Nietzsche believes reason is used to legitimise power. He believes reason must be resisted and defeated.

Nietzsche's fourth essay criticises language as a product of power. He believes language creates truth, not communicates it. Nietzsche argues that language explains one's will to power. Language must be overcome, he says.

The book's takeaways and life lessons are:

• "Master morality" and "slave morality," where powerful individuals have their own values and inferior people follow their oppressors.
• Rejecting conventional morality and examining its foundations in power and vengeance
• The concept of eternal repetition, termed as amor fati (literally "love of fate")
• The questioning of good and evil and "the good" as a philosophical principle
• Challenging traditional God ideas and religious morality
• The claim that "truth" is invented rather than discovered.
• The claim that society, politics, and the state stifle individual freedom and innovation and should be criticised.
• Against "herd mentality" and the need for self-confidence and self-control.
• Admitting one's wishes and rejecting self-denial and self-sacrifice to find happiness.
• The importance of daily self-mastery and transcendence.

CHAPTER LXXXIX

"Letters from a Stoic" by Seneca.

"Letters from a Stoic" is Seneca's correspondence with Lucilius. Seneca wrote to Lucilius. The letters discuss Stoicism, the soul, morality, wisdom, self-control, and the world. Seneca emphasises inner tranquilly, living in harmony with nature, and accepting the unchangeable in his texts.

The book emphasises the Stoic idea of accepting what cannot be changed and focusing on what can. Seneca urges his buddy to focus on the present and live in harmony with nature rather than fighting it. Wisdom and self-control, he believes, are crucial to inner peace and harmony.

The text also emphasises morality. Seneca believes that morality can only be achieved through following reason and virtue, not rules or laws. He also emphasises living a simple, moral life and avoiding wealth's temptations.

The book also discusses the universe and human spirit. Seneca believes the soul is immortal and that a reasonable and benign principle rules the universe. He also advises his friend to seek wisdom and comprehension of the universe, which he believes are necessary to inner calm.

Seneca's "Letters from a Stoic" explores Stoic philosophy, morality, wisdom, self-control, and the universe. It summarises Seneca's "Letters from a Stoic." Readers are advised to live in harmony with nature, accept what they cannot change, focus on the present, and seek inner peace.

The book's takeaways and life lessons are:

• The Stoic notion that one should accept life's occurrences and not let them affect one's mood.
• Self-control and self-discipline in moral living
• The belief that true wisdom includes admitting and accepting one's flaws.
• The importance of living in harmony with nature.
• The belief that emotional and mental detachment is the only way to reach true freedom.
• How to overcome fears to live a happy and prosperous life.
• The belief that one's character, not worldly possessions, determines true prosperity.
• The importance of living a simple, unadorned life without the complexity and extravagances of wealth and luxury.
• The conviction that only a good existence in harmony with nature and the environment can bring true happiness.

CHAPTER XC

“Meditations” by Marcus Aurelius

"Meditations" was written by Roman Emperor Marcus Aurelius. Each of the 12 books comprises brief, numbered parts on topics like philosophy, ethics, and personal growth.

In the book, Marcus reflects on his life and the Stoic philosophy he follows. He emphasises living in harmony with nature and reason and encourages the reader to live in the now rather than worrying about the past or future. He emphasises living in harmony with nature and reason. He also emphasises virtue, self-discipline, and self-control.

"Meditations" emphasises the idea that one can only discover true happiness and fulfilment within themselves. Marcus advises the reader to look within for true contentment rather than outside. He also emphasises the need of accepting life’s events as we can’t control them.

"Meditations" also addresses living well. Marcus emphasises living in harmony with nature and reason and encourages the reader to practise wisdom, justice, courage, and moderation. He advises readers to be humble, self-controlled, and simple.

"Meditations" is a classic because of its astute observations on human nature. It aids self-reflection, personal growth, and ethical, fulfilling living.

The book’s takeaways and life lessons are:

• The importance of reflection and self-improvement to live a life worth emulating; the need to accept one’s own transience and the world's transience to find true contentment; and the use of appreciation and mindfulness in daily life to achieve contentment.

- The importance of maintaining a lifestyle in harmony with nature and reason
- Stoicism, which involves accepting those aspects of one's life that one cannot change and being resolute in one's efforts to change those aspects over which one does have control; the practise of focusing one's attention on the here and now rather than being overly preoccupied with the past or future
- The necessity of self-discipline and the ability to regulate one's feelings and behaviour in difficult situations.

CHAPTER XCI

“Man's Search for Meaning” by Viktor Frankl

"Man’s Search for Meaning" was written by Holocaust survivor and psychiatrist Viktor Frankl. Frankl wrote this memoir on his Holocaust experiences and his thoughts on pain and survival. The book is divided into two parts: Frankl’s personal memoir of his time in concentration camps and a theoretical assessment of his experiences‘ psychological and philosophical ramifications. "Man’s Search for Meaning" has both parts.

Frankl believes the most basic human motive is the search for meaning. Even in the Holocaust, he believes people may find meaning in their suffering. He also believes that finding significance gives people hope and the will to live.

This book’s most significant notion is Frankl’s "logotherapy" psychotherapy. Logotherapy holds that the core human drive is meaning, contrary to traditional psychoanalysis’ belief that pleasure is the main motivation. Frankl believed that the quest for meaning was the most powerful force in human life and could overcome any situation.

"Tragic optimism" is another literary principle. Despite agonising agony, humans can still retain hope and optimism. Frankl believes that humans can find meaning in their suffering and endure even the worst conditions. He claims this ability allows humans to withstand even the worst situations.

The book also discusses personal responsibility and human

spirit. Frankl believed that people can choose their attitude and response to every situation, which can greatly impact their experience. He also emphasises the importance of accepting personal responsibility for one's actions and decisions as a prerequisite for true freedom and full potential.

"Man's Search for Meaning" examines human pain and survival. It illuminates the importance of finding purpose in life, the human spirit, and the role of individual agency in shaping our experiences.

The book's takeaways and life lessons are:

- This book recounts the author's time as a concentration camp prisoner during the Holocaust and how he found meaning in life despite his hardships.
- Frankl believes that the search for meaning is part of the human experience and that one can find purpose in life despite difficult circumstances.
- He proposes logotherapy, which seeks significance in life to relieve mental and emotional anguish. 1920s Carl Rogers invented logotherapy.
- Frankl emphasises taking responsibility for one's life and attitude even in the face of insurmountable obstacles.
- He also emphasises the importance of meaningful relationships, happiness, and purpose.
- Frankl's book teaches readers how to overcome life's problems and find meaning.

CHAPTER XCII

"The Freedom from the Known" by Jiddu Krishnamurti

"The Freedom from the Known" by Jiddu Krishnamurti examines the ego and human condition. The author invites readers to analyse their own beliefs and views and see beyond their mental bounds to better understand themselves and the world around them.

Krishnamurti believed that true freedom can only be achieved through trusting in the unknown. He believes that society, culture, and one's past experiences condition the mind, causing emotions of estrangement and disconnection. Before achieving full freedom, people must eliminate these limiting thoughts and beliefs.

The author emphasises self-awareness and mindfulness for emancipation. He encourages people to examine their thoughts and feelings and question their beliefs. He also stresses the importance of living in the present rather than worrying about the past or future.

he author also believes that true freedom comes from inside and cannot be obtained by pursuing external ambitions.

"The Freedom from the Known" invites readers to confront their beliefs, be present, and let go of the known to better understand themselves and the world.

The book's takeaways and life lessons are:

• The book encourages readers to think for themselves rather than following tradition to better understand themselves and the world.

• Krishnamurti believed that one must free themselves from the known—past experiences, ideas, and conditioning—to achieve true freedom.

This book encourages self-awareness, observation, and cognitive and emotional understanding.

• Krishnamurti emphasises remaining in the present rather than thinking about the past or future.

• The author emphasises self-discovery over external remedies.

• Krishnamurti believed that the genuine revolution is a personal change, not a political or social change.

• The author encourages readers to rethink their own beliefs and investigate new ideas before accepting them. The author also recommends readers to research ideas before accepting them.

• Krishnamurti advises readers to free themselves from ego and social conditioning to achieve true freedom and understanding.

CHAPTER XCIII

“On the Shortness of Life” by Seneca

Seneca’s "On the Shortness of Life" is a classic Stoic essay on how to maximise our time on Earth. Seneca believes most people chase fleeting pleasures and let their anxieties and desires rule them. He believes that living a meaningful life requires inner peace and focus on the important things. Seneca’s philosophy emphasises living in harmony with nature. He believes that living in connection with nature might help us overcome our worries and pleasures and find true inner peace. Another important premise is that we should focus on the now and not the past or future. Seneca advises living in the present to fully appreciate life’s beauty and mystery.

Seneca emphasises virtue and good judgement in his works. If we cultivate virtue, intelligence, and happiness, we can improve. He also stresses the importance of a simple, frugal, and focused life.

eneca provides practical advice on how to live a full life in addition to these ideas. He advises readers to set aside time to reflect, practise self-discipline, and serve others. He also asks readers to be open to learning from others.

In conclusion, Seneca’s "On the Shortness of Life" is a significant and thought-provoking work that offers timeless counsel on living a worthwhile life. It emphasises living in tune with nature, being present, fostering virtue and wisdom, and living a simple, selfless life. This book helps us overcome our anxieties and cravings to find true inner peace and pleasure.

The book's takeaways and life lessons are:

- Recognize that time is precious.
- Be mindful of our time and prioritise the most critical tasks.
- Focus on your goals and avoid distractions.
- Moderation and simplicity in all we do.
- Learn to ignore short-term pleasures to focus on long-term goals.
- Accept that our lives are short and use that realisation to enjoy each day to the fullest.
- Recognize that some things are beyond our control and focus on those we can affect.
- Develop wisdom and morality for a meaningful existence.

CHAPTER XCIV

"The Socrates Express: In Search of Life Lessons from Dead Philosophers" by Eric Weiner.

"The Socrates Express: In Search of Life Lessons from Dead Philosophers" by Eric Weiner examines the teachings of many philosophers and how they might be applied to modern life. Each chapter of this book covers a different philosopher and their core ideas.

Self-reflection and self-awareness are central to the text. Weiner emphasises the importance of self-reflection to comprehend and grow. He follows Socrates' thought that a happy life involves continually questioning one's beliefs and actions.

The book also discusses the importance of being present in life. Weiner references the Stoics, who believed one should focus on the present rather than the past or future. He also describes "ataraxia," a state of inner calm and freedom from disturbance achieved via mindfulness.

Weiner emphasises meaningful living and finding one's passion throughout the book. He quotes Epicurus, who believed that a happy life was simple and focused on pleasure and avoiding misery. He also discusses "eudaimonia," a state of happiness and fulfilment that one might achieve by living well and reaching their potential.

"The Socrates Express: In Search of Living Lessons from Dead Philosophers" is a synopsis of "In Search of Life Lessons from Dead Philosophers," which examines the teachings of many philosophers and how they might be applied to modern life. The author encourages self-reflection and self-awareness, living in the present, living a meaningful life, and finding their passion.

The book's takeaways and life lessons are:

• The author emphasises self-reflection and questioning to better understand oneself and the world. He follows Socrates' view that true wisdom comes from admitting ignorance.
• The author examines the Stoic philosophy of living in the present, which emphasises not worrying about the past or future. The author discusses this school's core tenet. He follows Seneca's concept that life is best lived in the present and accepting one's situation.
• "The Power of Humility" discusses humility and the importance of knowing one's boundaries. He believes modesty is the foundation of all virtues, following Confucius.
• This chapter discusses virtue and values. "The Importance of Living Virtuously" is the chapter title. Aristotle taught that virtue is living in accordance with reason and the good in the world, and he builds his reasoning on this. He reinforces this.
• To demonstrate their importance, the author examines community and relationships. He follows Epicurus' advice to surround oneself with like-minded individuals to be happy.

CHAPTER XCV

“The Big Question of Life” by Om Swami.

Om Swami’s "The Big Question of Life" examines life’s purpose and significance. Om Swami, a spiritual teacher and meditation master, has studied Eastern wisdom traditions for years. He wrote this book. In this book, he presents the most comprehensive approach to understanding life’s most pressing issues, drawing from a number of philosophic and theological traditions.

This study emphasises the importance of self-awareness. The author emphasises the importance of recognising one’s own thoughts, feelings, and actions and how they affect one’s view of the world. His point is that self-awareness is the first step to enlightenment because it unlocks the secrets of existence and is the first step in the journey.

The book explores non-attachment as a principle. The author claims that we must let rid of worldly possessions, other people’s approval, and our own egos to find true freedom and pleasure. He believes that practising non-attachment daily can lead to inner peace and freedom from want and pain.

The author explores mindfulness and how it might help one become more present. He says being more aware of our thoughts and emotions might help us be more present and appreciate life’s beauty. Mindfulness allows this.

The author also explores detachment and how it might interrupt the cycle of want and misery. The author also advises living in the present, becoming self-aware and observant, and letting go of attachments to material possessions, external validation, and one's ego to live a meaningful life.

"The Big Question of Existence" is a thought-provoking and enlightening book about existence and humankind. The author's approach is comprehensive, drawing from a variety of religious and philosophical ideas and offering practical suggestions on how to live a more fulfilling life.

The book's takeaways and life lessons are:

• The belief that one must conquer their ego and connect with a greater power to find happiness and fulfilment. Self-concept.

• The importance of self-awareness and mind-understanding to understand reality.

• The idea that everything in the universe is interconnected and entwined in a web of cause and effect, and that our actions and thoughts affect the environment around us and the universe itself.

• Karma is the belief that our actions affect our future.

• The need of cultivating compassion and empathy towards others to live a meaningful and satisfying life for oneself and one's community.

CHAPTER XCVI

"Siddhartha" by Hermann Hesse

In Hermann Hesse's novel "Siddhartha," a young man named Siddhartha searches for life's purpose. Novel protagonist Siddhartha. In ancient India, Siddhartha leaves his Brahmin life to pursue asceticism and then worldly pleasures.

Siddhartha learns about Buddhism, Hinduism, and other religions from the Buddha and Vasudeva. He also goes through many situations that shape him. He was a wealthy trader and friends with Govinda.

The book's main theme is that one may only gain true wisdom and enlightenment via self-discovery and personal experience. Siddhartha learns from the book that enlightenment is a convoluted path that requires patience, fortitude, and an open mind.

The book also discusses detachment. Siddhartha realises that true happiness can only be found by letting go of material possessions and focusing on the now. He also realises that true wisdom comes from accepting the transience of existence and the inevitability of change.

The story explores balancing and harmony. Siddhartha realises that true wisdom comes from balancing the spiritual and material, which is necessary for a happy and fulfilling existence. He realises that true wisdom comes from accepting and balancing one's positive and unfavourable traits.

"Siddhartha" follows one man's search for life's meaning and the lessons he learns. It also recounts his life lessons. This book explores self-discovery, detachment, balance, harmony, and enlightenment.

The book's takeaways and life lessons are:

• Self-knowledge and introspection are essential to happiness.
• The concept of a "eternal self" and the assumption that public procedures cannot provide true understanding.
• The dangers of attachment and desire and the importance of letting go of material items and social expectations to achieve enlightenment.
• The belief that only life experience and deliberate contemplation can provide true wisdom and understanding.
• balancing one's inner truth and intuition with society's customs and standards.
• The "Middle Way" to enlightenment balances and avoids extremes.
• That true enlightenment is a process of self-exploration and development, not a condition.
• The importance of living in the present and being fully attentive of one's actions and thoughts.
• The concept that inner serenity and contentment bring true happiness, not external circumstances or material possessions.
• The belief that one should seek unification and harmony with the universe and break free from the cycle of birth, life, and death.

CHAPTER XCVII

"The Art of War" by Sun Tzu

Sun Tzu's "The Art of War" is considered one of the best military strategy and tactics manuals. It is believed to have been written in ancient China and has been studied and used in business, sports, and politics. This book covers military planning, positioning, and tactics in thirteen chapters.

"The Art of War" teaches readers how important it is to understand and adapt to one's enemy's strengths and weaknesses, how important flexibility and speed in fighting are, and how powerful deception and surprise can be. Sun Tzu also emphasises knowing the topographical, climate, political, and economic aspects that may affect a combat.

"The Art of War" promotes "winning without fighting." Sun Tzu believed that nonviolent victories were the most important. He believes a smart leader should use diplomacy and strategy to win over the enemy's soldiers and leaders before using force. In business, companies try to outwit and outmanoeuvre their competitors rather than control or subdue them.

"The Art of War" also emphasises understanding the enemy's goals and concerns. Sun Tzu advised leaders to study their opponents' strengths and weaknesses and exploit their defences. He also emphasises maintaining good connections with friends and being mindful of political and economic factors that may lead to conflict.

In conclusion, Sun Tzu's "The Art of War" is a timeless strategy and military tactics manual. It emphasises preparation, positioning, strategy, and the importance of knowing and responding to the opponent's strengths and weaknesses, flexibility and speed in battle, and deception and surprise. It emphasises the need of knowing the terrain, climate, political, and economic factors that may influence a conflict. This book's main themes can be applied to business, athletics, and politics.

The book's takeaways and life lessons are:

- Understanding the opponent and geography is crucial. Sun Tzu emphasises the need of knowing the enemy and terrain to win battles.
- Flexibility and adaptability Sun Tzu emphasises adaptability and flexibility.
- Sun Tzu's "The Art of War" emphasises the need to outwit and outmanoeuvre opponents.
- Sun Tzu discusses how good leadership and communication may boost army morale.
- Knowledge and intellect matter Sun Tzu emphasises the importance of gathering information and insight to have a competitive edge.
- Speed and timing matter: In "The Art of War," Sun Tzu outlines how speed and timing can achieve strategic goals and gain an advantage in warfare.
- Sun Tzu emphasises resource optimization and avoiding unnecessary spending. "Economy of force" describes this.
- Sun Tzu examines surprise's strategic and tactical usefulness. He explains how surprise can achieve strategic goals.
- Upholding morality: Sun Tzu's "The Art of War" describes how morality can give a fighter an edge.
- Sun Tzu emphasises the need of knowing one's own and one's opponent's power.

CHAPTER XCVIII

"Peace Is Every Step: The Path of Mindfulness in Everyday Life" by Thich Nhat Hanh

"Peace Is Every Step" by Thich Nhat Hanh explores mindfulness and its role in finding inner peace and pleasure. The author, a Buddhist monk and peace campaigner, teaches readers how to practise mindfulness through breathing, walking, and dishwashing. Buddhist peace campaigner, author. He emphasises living in the now and being mindful of one's thoughts, feelings, and actions to increase compassion, understanding, and contentment.

The book's central thesis is that peace can only be realised in the present. The author recommends readers to focus on their current thoughts and actions rather than the past or future. He also recommends people to pay attention to their surroundings and appreciate nature, which can help them find peace and tranquilly. His book says this.

Interbeing, the idea that everything is connected and depends on everything else, is another important topic in the book. He also emphasises awareness in communication, encouraging readers to listen deeply and communicate honestly to build relationships.

The author also stresses self-compassion and self-care. He believes that self-care activities like going to the gym, meditating, and spending time outside can improve one's physical and mental health, which can boost happiness and fulfilment.

"Peace Is Every Step" guides readers through mindfulness

practises to attain inner peace, happiness, and fulfilment. It emphasises the importance of being present in the moment, being aware of one's thoughts, feelings, and actions, and being compassionate and understanding towards others. This book encourages self-compassion, self-care, and nature appreciation. Readers can understand and apply the book's principles because it's written simply.

The book's takeaways and life lessons are:

• Mindfulness is paying attention to the present moment without judgement or being distracted by external stimuli. Hanh recommends slow, deep breathing, contemplative walking, and deliberate eating to increase awareness.
• Interbeing is realising that everything is interconnected and interdependent. Readers are taught to recognise the interdependence of all living things and the natural world and live in a way that harms others the least.
• Five Mindfulness Trainings: The Five Mindfulness Trainings help Hanh live more mindfully and ethically. They're:
1. Respect for Life: protecting one's own and others' lives.
2. The only way to true happiness is to give up destructive habits.
3. Implementing Love is kindness, compassion, joy, and inclusion.
4. Open, Compassionate Communication and Deep Listening:
5. Nourishment and Healing: mindful eating and cultivating attention, focus, and insight for growth.
• The importance of nature: Hanh advises his readers to spend time in nature to find creativity, healing, and peace.

CHAPTER XCIX

"The Last Lecture" by Randy Pausch

"The Last Lecture," Randy Pausch's memoir, recounts his life and lessons as a computer science professor. The book was written by a terminally ill author. Pausch's Carnegie Mellon University speech inspired this book. He talked on living a meaningful life and achieving childhood dreams.

Each chapter covers a different aspect of Pausch's life and lessons. The book emphasises several life lessons and guiding ideas. These include the importance of having a family, friends, and community, having an optimistic attitude and sense of humour in the face of hardship, and working hard, persevering, and achieving one's goals.

Pausch emphasises living in the now and making the most of one's time rather than worrying about the past or future. He encourages others to pursue their passions and never give up on their dreams.

The book stresses the importance of "seizing the day" and making the most of every moment. Pausch advises readers to live purposefully and not waste time on unimportant things. He also emphasises assisting others and contributing to society.

"The Last Lecture" is an inspiring book on life and the importance of savouring every moment. It reminds us that we can influence the world and should live meaningful lives.

The book's takeaways and life lessons are:

- Pausch advises readers to live in the present and take every opportunity to maximise each day. Despite having a deadly condition, he found joy and meaning by focusing on the present and appreciating each day. He focused on the now.
- Find joy in the trip: Pausch emphasises finding joy in the journey rather than just the destination. He advises readers to enjoy the process rather than the result.
- Be passionate and persistent: Pausch advises being passionate and persistent to achieve goals. He encourages readers to work hard, be true to themselves, and persevere.
- Live a life of service: Pausch emphasises the importance of living a life of service and encourages readers to positively impact the world through volunteer work, mentorship, and other contributions.
- Always be honest: Pausch emphasises the importance of honesty, especially in difficult situations, throughout his discussion. He encourages readers to be their best selves and committed to their values.

CHAPTER C

"A Guide to the Good Life: The Ancient Art of Stoic Joy" by William B. Irvine

"A Guide to the Good Life: The Ancient Art of Stoic Joy" is a book by philosopher William B. Irvine that presents an introduction to the ancient philosophy of Stoicism and how it can be applied in modern life. The book is divided into four parts.

In the first part, Irvine provides an overview of the history of Stoicism and the key principles of the philosophy. He explains the Stoic approach to living a good life, which involves cultivating virtue and developing an inner sense of tranquility and contentment.

In the second part, Irvine discusses the practical techniques that the Stoics used to achieve this state of mind. He provides guidance on how to apply these techniques in modern life, including techniques such as negative visualization, self-denial, and mindfulness.

In the third part, Irvine examines the potential objections to Stoicism and addresses common misconceptions about the philosophy. He argues that Stoicism is not a cold, emotionless philosophy, but rather a practical and effective approach to living a fulfilling life.

In the final part, Irvine explores the idea of "Stoic joy" and how it relates to the pursuit of a good life. He shows how the Stoic approach can help individuals find happiness and meaning in their lives, even in the face of adversity.

Overall, "A Guide to the Good Life" provides an accessible

and practical introduction to Stoicism, making it a useful resource for anyone interested in applying this ancient philosophy to modern life.

The book's takeaways and life lessons are:

- Negative visualisation: Imagine worst-case scenarios and how you would handle them. This can teach you gratitude and prepare you for future struggles.
- Self-denial: Say "no" to junk food and impulse buys occasionally. This improves discipline and willpower.
- Mindfulness: Focus on the present and be completely involved. This might help you appreciate the little things and lessen tension and worry.
- Resilience: Focus on what you can control and accept the rest. This can bring serenity and relieve suffering.
- Be grateful for what you have. This can boost happiness and lessen envy and jealousy.
- Before reacting, assess your emotions. This helps you handle difficult situations.
- Focus on virtue: Instead than pursuing wealth, power, or fame, cultivate virtue and character. This can help you live your values-based life.

9 798889 864653

Printed by Libri Plureos GmbH in Hamburg, Germany